Kim Jong Il

MODERN WORLD LEADERS

Michelle Bachelet
Tony Blair
George W. Bush
Felipe Calderón
Hugo Chávez
Jacques Chirac
Hu Jintao
Hamid Karzai
Ali Khamenei
Kim Jong II
Thabo Mbeki

Angela Merkel
Hosni Mubarak
Pervez Musharraf
Ehud Olmert
Pope Benedict XVI
Pope John Paul II
Roh Moo Hyun
Vladimir Putin
The Saudi Royal Family
Ariel Sharon
Viktor Yushchenko

MODERN WORLD LEADERS

Kim Jong Il

Richard Worth

Kim Jong Il

Chelsea House
An imprint of Infobase Publishing
132 West 31st Street
New York, NY 10001

Library of Congress Cataloging-in-Publication Data
Worth, Richard.
  Kim Jong Il / Richard Worth.
    p. cm. — (Modern world leaders)
  Includes bibliographical references and index.
  ISBN 978-0-7910-9741-0 (hardcover)
  1. Korea (North)—History. 2. Korea (North)—Politics and government. 3. Kim, Chong-il, 1942- 4. Kim, Il-song, 1912-1994. I. Title. II. Series.
  DS935.W67 2008
  951.9305'1092—dc22
  [B]   2008004877

Chelsea House books are available at special discounts when purchased in bulk quantities for businesses, associations, institutions, or sales promotions. Please call our Special Sales Department in New York at (212) 967-8800 or (800) 322-8755.

You can find Chelsea House on the World Wide Web at http://www.chelseahouse.com

Text design by Erik Lindstrom
Cover design by Takeshi Takahashi

Printed in the United States of America

Bang EJB 10 9 8 7 6 5 4 3 2 1

This book is printed on acid-free paper.

All links and Web addresses were checked and verified to be correct at the time of publication. Because of the dynamic nature of the Web, some addresses and links may have changed since publication and may no longer be valid.

TABLE OF CONTENTS

On Leadership

Leadership, it may be said, is really what makes the world go round. Love no doubt smoothes the passage; but love is a private transaction between consenting adults. Leadership is a public transaction with history. The idea of leadership affirms the capacity of individuals to move, inspire, and mobilize masses of people so that they act together in pursuit of an end. Sometimes leadership serves good purposes, sometimes bad; but whether the end is benign or evil, great leaders are those men and women who leave their personal stamp on history.

Now, the very concept of leadership implies the proposition that individuals can make a difference. This proposition has never been universally accepted. From classical times to the present day, eminent thinkers have regarded individuals as no more than the agents and pawns of larger forces, whether the gods and goddesses of the ancient world or, in the modern era, race, class, nation, the dialectic, the will of the people, the spirit of the times, history itself. Against such forces, the individual dwindles into insignificance.

So contends the thesis of historical determinism. Tolstoy's great novel *War and Peace* offers a famous statement of the case. Why, Tolstoy asked, did millions of men in the Napoleonic Wars, denying their human feelings and their common sense, move back and forth across Europe slaughtering their fellows? "The war," Tolstoy answered, "was bound to happen simply because it was bound to happen." All prior history determined it. As for leaders, they, Tolstoy said, "are but the labels that serve to give a name to an end and, like labels, they have the least possible connection with the event." The greater the leader, "the more conspicuous the inevitability and the predestination of every act he commits." The leader, said Tolstoy, is "the slave of history."

Determinism takes many forms. Marxism is the determinism of class. Nazism the determinism of race. But the idea of men and women as the slaves of history runs athwart the deepest human instincts. Rigid determinism abolishes the idea of human freedom—the assumption of free choice that underlies every move we make, every word we speak, every thought we think. It abolishes the idea of human responsibility, since it is manifestly unfair to reward or punish people for actions that are by definition beyond their control. No one can live consistently by any deterministic creed. The Marxist states prove this themselves by their extreme susceptibility to the cult of leadership.

More than that, history refutes the idea that individuals make no difference. In December 1931, a British politician crossing Fifth Avenue in New York City between 76th and 77th streets around 10:30 P.M. looked in the wrong direction and was knocked down by an automobile—a moment, he later recalled, of a man aghast, a world aglare: "I do not understand why I was not broken like an eggshell or squashed like a gooseberry." Fourteen months later an American politician, sitting in an open car in Miami, Florida, was fired on by an assassin; the man beside him was hit. Those who believe that individuals make no difference to history might well ponder whether the next two decades would have been the same had Mario Constasino's car killed Winston Churchill in 1931 and Giuseppe Zangara's bullet killed Franklin Roosevelt in 1933. Suppose, in addition, that Lenin had died of typhus in Siberia in 1895 and that Hitler had been killed on the western front in 1916. What would the twentieth century have looked like now?

For better or for worse, individuals do make a difference. "The notion that a people can run itself and its affairs anonymously," wrote the philosopher William James, "is now well known to be the silliest of absurdities. Mankind does nothing save through initiatives on the part of inventors, great or small, and imitation by the rest of us—these are the sole factors in human progress. Individuals of genius show the way, and set the patterns, which common people then adopt and follow."

Leadership, James suggests, means leadership in thought as well as in action. In the long run, leaders in thought may well make the greater difference to the world. "The ideas of economists and political philosophers, both when they are right and when they are wrong," wrote John Maynard Keynes, "are more powerful than is commonly understood. Indeed the world is ruled by little else. Practical men, who believe themselves to be quite exempt from any intellectual influences, are usually the slaves of some defunct economist. . . . The power of vested interests is vastly exaggerated compared with the gradual encroachment of ideas."

But, as Woodrow Wilson once said, "Those only are leaders of men, in the general eye, who lead in action. . . . It is at their hands that new thought gets its translation into the crude language of deeds." Leaders in thought often invent in solitude and obscurity, leaving to later generations the tasks of imitation. Leaders in action—the leaders portrayed in this series—have to be effective in their own time.

And they cannot be effective by themselves. They must act in response to the rhythms of their age. Their genius must be adapted, in a phrase from William James, "to the receptivities of the moment." Leaders are useless without followers. "There goes the mob," said the French politician, hearing a clamor in the streets. "I am their leader. I must follow them." Great leaders turn the inchoate emotions of the mob to purposes of their own. They seize on the opportunities of their time, the hopes, fears, frustrations, crises, potentialities. They succeed when events have prepared the way for them, when the community is awaiting to be aroused, when they can provide the clarifying and organizing ideas. Leadership completes the circuit between the individual and the mass and thereby alters history.

It may alter history for better or for worse. Leaders have been responsible for the most extravagant follies and most monstrous crimes that have beset suffering humanity. They have also been vital in such gains as humanity has made in individual freedom, religious and racial tolerance, social justice, and respect for human rights.

There is no sure way to tell in advance who is going to lead for good and who for evil. But a glance at the gallery of men and women in MODERN WORLD LEADERS suggests some useful tests.

One test is this: Do leaders lead by force or by persuasion? By command or by consent? Through most of history leadership was exercised by the divine right of authority. The duty of followers was to defer and to obey. "Theirs not to reason why/Theirs but to do and die." On occasion, as with the so-called enlightened despots of the eighteenth century in Europe, absolutist leadership was animated by humane purposes. More often, absolutism nourished the passion for domination, land, gold, and conquest and resulted in tyranny.

The great revolution of modern times has been the revolution of equality. "Perhaps no form of government," wrote the British historian James Bryce in his study of the United States, *The American Commonwealth*, "needs great leaders so much as democracy." The idea that all people should be equal in their legal condition has undermined the old structure of authority, hierarchy, and deference. The revolution of equality has had two contrary effects on the nature of leadership. For equality, as Alexis de Tocqueville pointed out in his great study *Democracy in America*, might mean equality in servitude as well as equality in freedom.

"I know of only two methods of establishing equality in the political world," Tocqueville wrote. "Rights must be given to every citizen, or none at all to anyone . . . save one, who is the master of all." There was no middle ground "between the sovereignty of all and the absolute power of one man." In his astonishing prediction of twentieth-century totalitarian dictatorship, Tocqueville explained how the revolution of equality could lead to the *Führerprinzip* and more terrible absolutism than the world had ever known.

But when rights are given to every citizen and the sovereignty of all is established, the problem of leadership takes a new form, becomes more exacting than ever before. It is easy to issue commands and enforce them by the rope and the stake, the concentration camp and the *gulag*. It is much harder to use argument and achievement to overcome opposition and win consent. The Founding Fathers of the United States understood the difficulty. They believed that history had given them the opportunity to decide, as Alexander Hamilton wrote in the first Federalist Paper, whether men are indeed capable of basing government on "reflection and choice, or whether they are forever destined to depend . . . on accident and force."

Government by reflection and choice called for a new style of leadership and a new quality of followership. It required leaders to be responsive to popular concerns, and it required followers to be active and informed participants in the process. Democracy does not eliminate emotion from politics; sometimes it fosters demagoguery; but it is confident that, as the greatest of democratic leaders put it, you cannot fool all of the people all of the time. It measures leadership by results and retires those who overreach or falter or fail.

It is true that in the long run despots are measured by results too. But they can postpone the day of judgment, sometimes indefinitely, and in the meantime they can do infinite harm. It is also true that democracy is no guarantee of virtue and intelligence in government, for the voice of the people is not necessarily the voice of God. But democracy, by assuring the right of opposition, offers built-in resistance to the evils inherent in absolutism. As the theologian Reinhold Niebuhr summed it up, "Man's capacity for justice makes democracy possible, but man's inclination to justice makes democracy necessary."

A second test for leadership is the end for which power is sought. When leaders have as their goal the supremacy of a master race or the promotion of totalitarian revolution or the acquisition and exploitation of colonies or the protection of greed and privilege or the preservation of personal power, it is likely that their leadership will do little to advance the cause of humanity. When their goal is the abolition of slavery, the liberation of women, the enlargement of opportunity for the poor and powerless, the extension of equal rights to racial minorities, the defense of the freedoms of expression and opposition, it is likely that their leadership will increase the sum of human liberty and welfare.

Leaders have done great harm to the world. They have also conferred great benefits. You will find both sorts in this series. Even "good" leaders must be regarded with a certain wariness. Leaders are not demigods; they put on their trousers one leg after another just like ordinary mortals. No leader is infallible, and every leader needs to be reminded of this at regular intervals. Irreverence irritates leaders but is their salvation. Unquestioning submission corrupts leaders and demeans followers. Making a cult of a leader is always a mistake. Fortunately hero worship generates its own antidote. "Every hero," said Emerson, "becomes a bore at last."

The single benefit the great leaders confer is to embolden the rest of us to live according to our own best selves, to be active, insistent, and resolute in affirming our own sense of things. For great leaders attest to the reality of human freedom against the supposed inevitabilities of history. And they attest to the wisdom and power that may lie within the most unlikely of us, which is why Abraham Lincoln remains the supreme example of great leadership. A great leader, said Emerson, exhibits new possibilities to all humanity. "We feed on genius. . . . Great men exist that there may be greater men."

Great leaders, in short, justify themselves by emancipating and empowering their followers. So humanity struggles to master its destiny, remembering with Alexis de Tocqueville: "It is true that around every man a fatal circle is traced beyond which he cannot pass; but within the wide verge of that circle he is powerful and free; as it is with man, so with communities." ●

1

Nuclear Showdown

ON OCTOBER 9, 2006, AN UNDERGROUND EXPLOSION OCCURRED IN NORTH Korea, a nation about the size of Mississippi, located along the east coast of Asia. The blast was monitored by the United States Air Force Technical Applications Center (AFTAC). This arm of the U.S. Department of Defense monitors nuclear explosions. AFTAC operates ground stations and aircraft that measure nuclear blasts and collect any material that reaches the atmosphere. The explosion, about the size of a small earthquake, had occurred at Yongbyon. This nuclear facility, located about 50 miles (80.5 kilometers) north of the capital, Pyongyang, is operated by North Korea's dictator, Kim Jong Il.

After carefully studying the explosion, scientists concluded that North Korea had, indeed, detonated its first nuclear blast. This explosion occurred several months after tests of intercontinental ballistic missiles by the North Korean government.

These missiles were fired off the coast of North Korea into the Sea of Japan. Referring to the nuclear tests, Graham Allison, a former U.S. Defense Department official, said, "I think this is bad news for the country, bad news for the region, bad news for the world."

Allison feared that other nations in Asia might want to develop nuclear weapons to protect themselves against a possible attack by the Communist government of North Korea. Currently only nine nations in the world have nuclear weapons capability. These include the United States, Russia, India, Pakistan, Israel, France, England, China, and now North Korea. If more nations obtain these weapons, the risk increases that they might be used in a nuclear war.

In addition, some experts feared that North Korea might be tempted to sell nuclear weapons to terrorist groups like al Qaeda. In the past, Kim Jong Il sold weapons to nations in the Middle East, including harsh dictatorships like Syria and Iran. As author Derek D. Smith wrote, "If you can't deter the terrorist organizations, you'd better be sure to deter whoever is supplying them." He was referring to North Korea.

After learning of the North Korean nuclear test, U.S. president George W. Bush reacted strongly. "The transfer of nuclear weapons or material by North Korea to states or non-state entities would be considered a grave threat to the United States," he said, "and we would hold North Korea fully accountable of the consequences of such action."

Experts disagree on why Kim Jong Il decided to conduct North Korea's first nuclear test. Some suggest that he was responding to a speech delivered in 2002 by President Bush. At that time, Bush said North Korea was part of the "axis of evil." These nations—which also included Iran and Iraq—were believed by President Bush to pose a grave threat to world peace. According to the *Economist*, Kim Jong Il believed that "if you do not want to be invaded by America, as was Iraq, then it is best to get your weapons of mass destruction up and

Bush branded North Korea part of the "axis of evil" because U.S. intelligence indicated that Kim was accelerating his nuclear weapons program.

running. Once your own security is assured, you can bargain from a position of strength."

President Bush branded North Korea part of the "axis of evil" because U.S. intelligence indicated that Kim was accelerating his nuclear weapons program. At the same time, the United States cut off oil shipments and other aid to North Korea. These shipments had started in the 1990s as part of an earlier agreement by the United States when North Korea agreed to stop its nuclear program. At that time, North Korea's government also allowed inspectors to enter the country to make sure that the agreement was not violated. When President Bush abruptly stopped the oil shipments in 2002, Kim Jong Il reacted immediately. He refused to allow international inspectors to return to his country to find out whether he was developing nuclear weapons.

While Kim's decision to resume the program may have been in response to President Bush's statements, some observers believe that far more was involved. Chinese professor Zhang Liangui, an expert in international relations, pointed out that North Korea had long been engaged in an effort to develop nuclear weapons. This program began in the 1950s, soon after North Korea became a Communist nation. Its purpose had been to strengthen the North Korean regime and protect it from possible invasion by South Korea or the United States. American forces invaded North Korea following its invasion of South Korea in 1949. This war devastated North Korea and left a lasting impression on its leaders. The resumption of the nuclear testing program in 2002 was simply a continuation of a long-standing policy of self-defense.

North Korean soldiers attend a mass rally celebrating the success of the country's first nuclear weapons test. A small country about the size of Mississippi, North Korea is one of the most militarized nations in the world. Its development and production of nuclear weapons concerns the international community because of fears that North Korean leader Kim Jong Il may be tempted to sell the arsenal to terrorist organizations.

RESPONDING TO THE NUCLEAR TEST

Ever since North Korea banned the nuclear inspectors in 2002, several nations have tried to persuade Kim to resume talks and end the weapons program. These nations include China, Russia, Japan, South Korea, and the United States. Their efforts took on a new sense of urgency following the nuclear test in October 2006. China, Russia, Japan, and South Korea are all nations located in the same region as North Korea, so a nuclear-armed government led by Kim Jong Il poses a grave threat to all of them.

During February 2007, delegates from these countries met in Beijing, the capital of China. Joining the discussions were representatives of the United States and North Korea. Kim Jong Il had indicated after the nuclear test that he was prepared to discuss an end to the North Korean program in return for economic aid. This led some experts to believe that the purpose of the test all along had been to force the rest of the world to take notice of North Korea and to give Kim what he wanted. North Korea is a very poor nation that has suffered from famine and drought in the past. As a result, it depends heavily on aid from abroad. Much of this aid has come from China and South Korea as well as the United States.

Following the nuclear blast, the United Nations voted to place economic penalties on North Korea. It required member nations to prevent North Korea from exporting weapons to any other countries. In addition, the UN stated that its members should not export luxury items—such as fine wines—to North Korea. Kim Jong Il reportedly enjoys these wines at the many parties he hosts inside his palaces in North Korea.

After several days of the six-party talks in Beijing, North Korea agreed to "shut down and seal for the purpose of eventual abandonment" its nuclear operations at Yongbyon. In return, the other nations agreed that the equivalent of $25 million in North Korean funds, held by a Chinese bank, could be released. These funds had reportedly been earned from illegal activities carried on by Kim Jong Il's government. In addition, North Korea would receive 50,000 tons of fuel oil. More oil and further economic aid would be delivered as inspectors examined the nuclear facilities to make sure that they had been completely "disabled."

After confirming that North Korea had tested a nuclear weapon, representatives from the United States, Japan, China, Russia, and South Korea met with North Korean officials in Beijing in 2007. U.S. envoy Christopher Hill *(above)* and delegates in attendance agreed to send food, oil, and economic aid to North Korea in return for their nuclear disarmament.

"The sooner they get these actions done, the sooner they get the fuel," said Christopher Hill, representing the United States at the Beijing talks. But Kim Jong Il did not move quickly to shut down the Yongbyon facility. According to the *Economist,* "his officials are said to have demanded privately that America instead recognize North Korea as a nuclear power." In other words, Kim Jong Il wanted to keep his current nuclear weapons. What's more, the Beijing agreement did not mention that North Korea must never renew its nuclear testing program in the future. This left open the question of whether Kim Jong Il could be completely trusted not to resume testing again.

By April 2007, little had happened to implement the agreement hammered out by the six nations at the talks in Beijing. Inspectors from the International Atomic Energy Agency (IAEA), an international body that monitors nuclear facilities, were supposed to have gone to Yongbyon. Kim was expected to have given the inspectors all the information they needed on his nuclear capabilities and then put a freeze on his operations. But none of these things had occurred. Finally in July, as fuel oil began to arrive from South Korea, North Korea announced that it had discontinued operations at its nuclear reactor in Yongbyon. Meanwhile, inspectors from the IAEA had arrived in North Korea to verify the statements made by North Korea.

Later in July, the six-party talks continued and more fuel oil arrived from South Korea. The next step was for Kim Jong Il to provide a complete list of his nuclear facilities so they could be inspected and eventually shut down. According to the *Economist,* "Mr. Kim denies that he has a uranium program." Nevertheless the government of Pakistan admitted that one of its scientists sold Kim equipment to manufacture nuclear weapons and he "has attempted to buy other related equipment on the black market [illegally]. This much America is sure of; what it doesn't know is what Mr. Kim has done with it all."

Finally in October, the six powers agreed on a plan to end North Korea's nuclear operations by the beginning of 2008. At the same time, South Korean president Roh Moo Hyun visited Pyongyang for a meeting with Kim Jong Il. According to the *New York Times,* "Pyongyang's usually drab sidewalks blossomed with color as North Koreans, dressed in their holiday best, waved pink and red paper flowers . . . [and] erupted into . . . chants of 'hurray' and 'unify the fatherland' as Mr. Roh rode through central Pyongyang in an open limousine." These demonstrations had been carefully arranged by the North Korean government. Roh had come to talk with Kim about reducing the size of his armies in return for South Korean aid to strengthen the North Korean economy.

As a result of summit talks over several days, South Korea agreed to provide some economic aid aimed at helping North Korea develop the port city of Haeju. President Roh also said that his government would continue a project begun in 2004, building factories in Kaesong, a North Korean city. These have already provided jobs for North Koreans. In return, Kim promised that he would dismantle his nuclear facilities at Yongbyon.

No one can be sure whether he will keep these promises. Perhaps the best estimate can be provided by examining the history of North Korea and understanding the personality of its unique ruler, Kim Jong Il.

2

Early Korea

KOREA, WHICH MEANS "THE LAND OF THE MORNING CALM," IS A PENINSULA about 600 miles (965.6 km) long that lies on the east coast of Asia. A large part of Korea is covered by long mountain ranges. These include the Chanbaek Mountains along the border with Korea's northern neighbor, Manchuria, and the T'aebaek Mountains that lie along the eastern coast near the Sea of Japan. Large rivers crisscross Korea, many of them emptying into the Yellow Sea—known as the West Sea in Korea—on the western coast of the peninsula near China.

The early history of Korea begins in 2333 B.C. when a leader named Tan-gun brought together many of the local tribes into the kingdom of Choson. This kingdom straddled the lands that make up Manchuria and modern-day North Korea. During the twelfth century B.C., Pyongyang—the current capital of North Korea—became the capital of the Choson kingdom. Throughout much of its history, Korea had to deal with a powerful Chinese empire on its borders. In 108 B.C., the Chinese invaded Korea and established colonies along the peninsula that lasted for approximately 400 years.

During the fourth century A.D., however, a new kingdom called Koguryŏ arose in southern Manchuria, invaded the Korean Peninsula, and drove out the Chinese. The two principle cities of the Koguryŏ kingdom were T'onggu, on the Yalu River along the border with Manchuria, and Pyongyang, located on the Taedong River. About the same time, two other strong kingdoms were growing in southern Korea: Shilla in the east and Paekche in the west.

Wars were constant among these three kingdoms, each of them trying to gain an advantage over the others to destroy them. Shilla allied itself with the Chinese empire, and together they launched a combined attack on Koguryŏ in 612. But the Chinese army, numbering one million soldiers, was defeated by Korean general Ŭlchi Mundŏk, who annihilated most of the enemy. Another invasion that occurred in 645 was also beaten back by the Koreans. According to Andrea Matles Savada, editor of *North Korea: A Country Study,* "Koreans have always viewed these victories as sterling examples of resistance to foreign aggression. Had Koguryŏ not beaten back the invaders, all the states of the peninsula might have fallen under extended Chinese domination."

SHILLA

Nevertheless, by the 660s, the wars had exhausted both Paekche and Koguryŏ, and Shilla became the major power along the Korean Peninsula. Kŭmsŏng, the capital of Shilla, was a large city with a population of about one million people, located in the eastern part of Korea. Buddhism was the religion of the people in Shilla. This religion had been introduced along the Korean Peninsula from China in the fourth century A.D.

Buddhism had been founded in the sixth century B.C. by Siddhartha Gautama—known as the Buddha—a nobleman born in Nepal. Buddhists believe in the Four Noble Truths, established by Siddhartha. According to these Truths, all life is suffering and this suffering is caused by our earthly desires, such as the need for power and physical pleasures that leave us unfulfilled. However, Siddhartha taught that these desires can be eliminated and that we can achieve a state of peace, or nirvana. But to do this, individuals must set themselves along the Noble Eightfold Path. This includes a life of virtue, meditation, and personal insight.

About the same time that Buddhism arrived in Korea, the teachings of Confucius also began to influence the Korean people. Born in the sixth century B.C., Confucius was a scholar and philosopher. He developed a system built on respect and obedience among children for their parents and subjects for their ruler. To earn this respect, parents and rulers had to exhibit the virtue of good leadership. Leaders were expected to be educated in the teachings of Confucius as well as in various other subjects, such as literature, mathematics, and foreign languages. Since there was no written Korean language in this period, educated Koreans were expected to master the Chinese language. Young people who wanted to serve in the Shilla government were required to pass a rigorous set of examinations to demonstrate their knowledge of all these subjects. A similar program had been established in China many years earlier. Indeed, the ideal individual in the Confucian system was a "learned scholar-official who was equally adept at poetry and statecraft."

NEW KINGDOMS

By the early tenth century, the power of Shilla had declined as a result of conflicts among the king and his aristocratic followers. A new leader named Wang Kŏn established a kingdom called Koryŏ, which eventually became known as Korea. Wang Kŏn defeated the armies of Shilla and unified the peninsula under a single ruler. The new king built a magnificent capital at the site of modern Kaesong in central Korea. According to author

Early Korean culture was influenced by the teachings of Confucius *(above)* who believed good leaders should be well educated in a variety of subjects and respectful of their parents.

Andrew Nahm, the capital included beautiful palaces, as well as magnificent Buddhist temples and government buildings. For defense, Kaesong was circled by huge stone walls, while another walled enclosure stretched around the king's palace.

A group of government officials trained in the Confucian system ran the country from the capital. They also served as local officials in the Korean countryside. These officials were mainly from well-to-do landowning families. The economy of the kingdom was based on agriculture, primarily rice and other crops, such as barley, spices, and fruits. The land was tilled and harvested by poor peasant families who worked for the landowners. In addition to agriculture, the government ran mining operations, digging gold, silver, and iron. The mining was done by Korean slaves who also worked in manufacturing operations, producing silk, paper, and pottery.

During the thirteenth century, China and Korea were invaded by the Mongols. These large armies of horsemen swept out of Mongolia led by Genghis Khan, destroying cities, killing the inhabitants, and spreading fear across Asia. In 1254, after marching down the Korean Peninsula, the Mongols took 200,000 prisoners and slaughtered many thousands more. They also forced the Korean king to turn over a large supply of gold, silver, and food for the Mongol armies. Meanwhile, the Mongols had established a kingdom in China, which was controlled by Emperor Kublai Khan.

After the emperor's death in 1294, however, the power of the Mongols in China began to decline during the next century. Meanwhile, in Korea, the Koryŏ king was eventually overthrown by a successful general, Yi Sŏng-gye. He established a new kingdom called Choson and a royal dynasty that would rule from 1392 until the early twentieth century.

THE YI DYNASTY

After General Yi's death in 1408, one of his sons, T'aejo, built a new capital for the kingdom at Seoul, the modern capital of

South Korea. Located near the Han River, Seoul lay in a large basin encircled by high mountains. Like most cities during this period, it was protected by a system of stone walls that could be defended by a large force of armed guards. Four gates—the East, the West, the South, and the North—provided entry into Seoul. While inside the city itself, the Yi rulers constructed palaces, beautiful gardens, and pavilions.

From Seoul, the bureaucrats—called the *yangban*—ran the government. More than at any time in the past, these Confucian trained scholars held power in Korea. According to author Andrew Nahm, this group of people "controlled politics, sustained social morality and ethics, and nurtured what became known as *yangban* culture. It seemed as though the entire society existed to support this class, which was barred from engaging in farming, manufacture, and commerce, as well as other professions. . . . The political and economic power of the *yangban* families was, in most cases, perpetuated by educational opportunities for the civil service examination which were limited almost exclusively to this class."

The yangban made up about 10 percent of the population, and along with the aristocrats, they were the most important people in Korea. Most Koreans, however, were fishermen or poor serfs who lived on the land owned by the aristocracy and harvested their crops. During the Yi dynasty, the population of Korea grew tremendously, expanding from about 3 million in the seventeenth century to almost 9 million two centuries later.

During the Yi period, Korea developed its own written language and no longer depended entirely on Chinese symbols. A unique type of poetry called *shijo*, which had first appeared during the Koryŏ era, flowered under the Yi dynasty. One of the best-known poets was Shin Hum—a yangban who served in the government during the late sixteenth and early seventeenth centuries. After leaving the government because he did not want to work for a king he believed to be incompetent, Shin Hum wrote:

> Do not laugh, foolish people
> Whether my roof beams are long or short or
> The pillars are crooked,
> The snail shell, my grass hut,
> The vines that cover it, the encircling hills
> And the bright moon above,
> Are mine, and mine alone.

During the same period that Shin Hum served in the government, Korea was invaded by powerful Japanese armies in 1592 and 1597. They planned to use the Korean Peninsula as an invasion route into China. Nevertheless, the Koreans, led by General Yi Sun-shin, managed to beat back the invasion with the help of the Chinese. But the war created havoc in Korea, destroying many acres of productive farmlands and reducing the food supply. A short time later, a rebellion occurred in China, overthrowing the ruling king. The victorious armies then decided to invade Korea to insure that it would be loyal to the new government. One poet, Kim Sang-hŏn, was captured by the Chinese and wrote, "I leave the mountains and rivers of my homeland/In these uncertain times/Who could tell that I might return."

DEALING WITH POWERFUL ENEMIES

Korea had become a pawn in a violent chess game between Japan and China for control of the peninsula. This pattern repeated itself again and again over the next three centuries.

Korea's weakness in the face of its powerful enemies gave rise to the Shirhak movement. The intellectuals who participated in the movement called on the Yi emperors to reform society, strengthen the army, and improve the government so they could deal with China and Japan. One scholar, Yu Hyŏng-won, wrote *Essay on Social Reform* urging the emperor to eliminate the class structure, bring equality to everyone, and give the peasants their own land. During the eighteenth century, Korean emperors attempted to eliminate corruption from the government and tried to develop new programs to help the poor.

But during the first half of the nineteenth century, weak emperors permitted corruption to increase, and many people lost confidence in the government. Throughout this same period, some Korean scholars had begun reading books from Europe. They learned about more advanced scientific ideas, economic programs, and military weapons, which were almost unknown in Korea. Meanwhile, Catholic missionaries from the West had already entered China. During the late eighteenth century, Catholic churches also began to appear in Korea.

Beginning in the early nineteenth century, however, there was a strong reaction among conservative government leaders against Western ideas. Many Catholics, for example, were rounded up and executed. Korea closed its doors to European ideas. It became known as the "hermit kingdom," closed to the outside world, except China and Japan.

The conservative reaction reached a high point in the 1860s during the reign of a 12-year-old king named Kojong. The real ruler of Korea was the emperor's father, Taewŏn-gun, a powerful prince who was determined to protect Korea from European influence. Over the previous decades, Taewŏn-gun had watched powerful European nations make increasing demands on China and Japan. Great Britain, for example, carried on a highly profitable trade in opium—a powerful drug—among the Chinese people. An estimated 2 million people were addicted to the drug. When the Chinese government opposed the trade, the British invaded China during the Opium War (1840–1842). As a result of a British victory, China was forced to accept the sale of opium by English merchants.

In 1866, an American merchant ship appeared off the coast of Korea near Pyongyang. When Korean officials told the ship's captain to leave, his crew came ashore. They began to steal food supplies from local stores and even ran off with several Korean women. In response, the Koreans stormed the ship and killed all the men on board. Although American diplomats tried to force the Koreans to pay for the loss of lives and property on the ship, Taewŏn-gun refused. In 1871, a small American force of a few hundred troops invaded Korea. The U.S. soldiers, with modern rifles and artillery, easily overwhelmed the Korean forces, who used primitive weapons. Although the American army had planned to capture Seoul, there were too few of them and they were forced to retreat by the Koreans.

While the Americans had failed to open up the "hermit kingdom," the Japanese were more successful. In 1875, they invaded Korea with a much stronger military expedition and forced the government to sign the Kanghwa Treaty. Under this agreement, Korea began to open its doors to Japanese merchants, who realized that the peninsula was an important market for their products. The Japanese established operations in the cities of Seoul, Pusan, and Inchon. During the early 1880s, Korea signed trade agreements with several Western governments, including the United States, Great Britain, and Germany. These nations were strong enough to force the Koreans into signing treaties that permitted Western merchants to sell their goods at very low tariffs (taxes imposed by a government on foreign products).

As a result of the agreements with the United States and other Western powers, Protestant missionaries also began coming to Korea. They established churches and hospitals and opened schools. Many of them came from America, including Dr. Horace N. Allen, a medical missionary who arrived in 1884. The following year, Dr. and Mrs. Horace G. Underwood, who were Presbyterians, arrived in Korea. After them came Methodist missionaries, who brought Christian hymns from Europe and the United States and introduced a Korean translation of the

Because of its unenviable geographic location between Japan and the rest of Asia, Korea often served as the battleground for skirmishes involving Japan, China, and Russia. The Koreans attempted to use diplomatic means to negotiate with the three countries, all of which wanted the peninsula for their own economic and defensive purposes. The photograph above, which dates from 1863, is believed to be the oldest dated photograph of Koreans.

Bible in 1900. Many Koreans joined the Protestant churches while others sent their children to the missionary schools. Among them was the family of North Korea's Communist ruler, Kim Il Sung, who took power in 1945.

THE DECLINE OF THE YI GOVERNMENT

Many Koreans were opposed to the presence of foreign merchants in their cities. In 1882, riots broke out in Seoul against the Japanese, some of whom were killed. To deal with the situation, the Chinese invaded Korea. They forced Taewón-gun to give up power and brought an end to the rioting. The Chinese were followed by a Japanese invasion. Japan forced the Korean government to pay a large amount of money for the destruction of Japanese property and the deaths of Japanese citizens during the riots. The government of King Kojong was too weak to resist.

Over the next decade, Japan and China struggled to gain the upper hand in Korea. The Japanese regarded Korea as "a dagger pointed at the heart of Japan," if it fell under the control of China or another foreign power. As a result, Japan kept pressuring the government to grant increased trade rights to Japanese merchants. In the meantime, the Chinese were also demanding more power for their traders on the Korean Peninsula. Indeed, their share of imports increased during the late 1880s, while Japan's declined. While this struggle was going on, economic conditions inside Korea had been growing worse. Poor harvests and drought led to massive unrest among the Korean peasants. By 1893, a peasant revolt, known as the Tonghak uprising, began sweeping the country.

To deal with the rebellion, King Kojong called in the Chinese. This was followed by a Japanese invasion of the peninsula and the outbreak of the Sino-Japanese War in 1894. Within a few months, the Japanese had defeated the Chinese armies, put down the Tonghak revolt, and taken control of Korea. But the rising power of Japan alarmed other governments who had an interest in the region. Russia was especially concerned when Japan forced China to give the Japanese control of the Liaotung Peninsula. Lying to the west of Korea, the Liaotung Peninsula was part of Manchuria. It offered the Japanese a port on the Yellow Sea that the Russians wanted for themselves.

THEY REALIZED THAT THEIR COUNTRY HAD LOST ITS INDEPENDENCE AND BECOME LITTLE MORE THAN A BATTLEGROUND FOR THE GREAT POWERS.

With help from France and Germany, who also feared the rising power of Japan, Russia forced the Japanese to give up Liaotung. Meanwhile, Russia sent its diplomats to Korea, where they hoped to reduce the power of the Japanese. They were welcomed by some members of the Korean government, who mistrusted Japan. Fearful that their own power was declining, the Japanese acted quickly. They assassinated Queen Min, the wife of King Kojong, in 1895. Queen Min had been an enemy of Japan and a strong supporter of the Chinese.

The struggle between Russia and Japan for control of the Korean government angered many Koreans. They realized that their country had lost its independence and become little more than a battleground for the great powers. During the 1890s, several Korean reformers joined together to form the Independence Club. They published the *Independent*, which called on Koreans to strengthen the government against foreign influence. In 1898, the Independence Club held a large conference in Seoul urging the government to reassert its independence from foreign control. However, King Kojong regarded the Independence Club as a threat to his government. Late in 1898, he ordered an end to the club, and its leaders quickly left Korea to avoid being arrested.

Following the end of the independence movement, the struggle between Russia and Japan continued. Early in 1904, the two nations went to war over control of Korea and the Liaodong Peninsula in Manchuria. During the Russo-Japanese War, Japan invaded Korea and rapidly marched into Seoul.

Japanese forces also defeated the Russians on the Liaodong Peninsula. As a result of a peace treaty signed in 1905, Japan became the major power in Korea. Two years later, Emperor Kojong abdicated his throne—that is, he gave up power—and Japan annexed Korea, making it part of the Japanese empire.

CHAPTER

3

Kim Il Sung and the Birth of North Korea

ON APRIL 15, 1912, TWO YEARS AFTER THE JAPANESE TOOK CONTROL OF Korea, Kim Song-ju was born in the town of Chilgol outside Pyongyang. As an adult, he would change his name to Kim Il Sung and become the ruler of North Korea for almost half a century.

Like many Koreans, Kim Il Sung's parents—his father, Kim Hyong-jik, and mother, Kang Pan-sok—were patriots who opposed the Japanese takeover of their country. "No feeling in the world is greater, more ennobling and more sacred than patriotism," Kim later said. Soon after the conquest, land that had belonged to Korean families for generations was taken by Japanese officials and given to farmers who had immigrated to Korea from Japan.

The Japanese also ordered that no Koreans could speak out against the new government, and all Korean newspapers were forced to stop publication.

Nevertheless, small groups of Korean patriots continued to meet and discuss methods of driving the Japanese out of Korea. Others fled to China, Manchuria, and the United States, where they started organizations dedicated to restoring an independent Korean government. These nationalists, as they were called, took heart from the policies of U.S. president Woodrow Wilson. In 1918, Wilson announced his Fourteen Points aimed at laying the foundation for world peace and bringing an end to World War I. This conflict had raged across Europe for the past four years. During the war, the Allies—Great Britain, France, Russia, and the United States—had battled the Central Powers—Germany, Austria-Hungary, and Turkey.

With the defeat of the Central Powers and the beginning of a peace conference in Paris in 1919, Koreans hoped that the victorious allies might force Japan to give up its control of Korea. At about the same time, the Korean emperor Kojong died, and rumors began to circulate that he had been murdered. A giant demonstration occurred in Seoul, which included the seven-year-old Kim Song-ju and his parents. "I shouted for independence standing on tiptoe, squeezed in between the adults," Kim later wrote.

But the Japanese acted swiftly, brutally putting down the demonstrations. Approximately 1,200 Koreans were killed and thousands more were wounded. Shortly afterward, Kim and his parents, along with many other Koreans, left their homeland and headed north to Manchuria. An unsettled frontier that was claimed by Chinese warlords, land was readily available in Manchuria for Koreans to settle. They could also continue to work against the Japanese government without being thrown into prison.

When he was 11 years old, Kim's father decided that his son must return to Korea. Kim Hyong-jik did not want the boy to forget about his homeland. Kim was sent to live with his grandfather, a teacher at Changdok School. As Kim attended classes at the school, he noticed that the students were required to learn Japanese as the national language. This was part of the government's policy to change Korea into a colony of the Japanese empire. "I asked my grandfather why the Japanese language book was titled *Mother-tongue Reader*," Kim said. "He merely heaved a sigh," because the Japanese were in charge and there was nothing he could do about it.

Kim also noticed how much poverty existed in the country-side. The Japanese had imported new irrigation methods and improved seeds to increase the rice harvest in Korea. But much of the surplus was sent to feed the people of Japan. The amount of rice available to the Koreans was cut in half by the Japanese during the 1920s and 1930s.

THE REVOLUTIONARY

Kim Song-ju returned to Manchuria in 1925, and soon afterward his father died. At 14, he was enrolled in another school that was run by Korean nationalists. By this time a split had occurred among Korean revolutionaries between Nationalists and Communists. In 1918, after a revolution that overthrew the Russian tsar, Communists had taken control of Russia and renamed it the Soviet Union. Led by Vladimir Lenin, the Communists had established a dictatorship in the Soviet Union based on the principles of Socialism. These principles included an end to the wealthy aristocracy and equality for the masses, under the control of the Communist Party. Communist organizations soon began to arise in Manchuria and China, and even inside Korea.

Kim spent only part of a year at the nationalist school before moving to Jilin, a Manchurian city. Although his mother had very little money, she somehow managed to pay for her son's tuition. In Jilin, one of Kim's closest friends was a Methodist minister, Reverend Sohn Jong-do. Kim was a guest at the home of Sohn and his wife, where he enjoyed many meals with them. Sohn's son recalled that Kim "was very enthusiastic on political and social problems." He worked at the Methodist chapel, directed plays, prayed with other members of the congregation, and played the organ.

In Jilin, Kim was influenced by one of the teachers, Shang Yue, a member of the Chinese Communist Party. Kim rapidly lost patience with the Nationalists. He believed that they were far more interested in arguing among themselves than in fighting the Japanese. Near the end of the 1920s, Kim helped organize a Communist youth group. But the Chinese warlords who were opposed to Communism arrested Kim and some of his friends in 1929. After refusing to talk to the authorities, they were finally released from prison in 1930. Reverend Sohn helped to secure his release by bribing the authorities in charge of the prison.

By the time he left prison, Kim wrote that he had become a committed revolutionary. He changed his name from Song-ju to Il Sung, which means "become the sun." In 1931, Kim Il Sung became a member of the Chinese Communist Party. During that same year, Japanese armies had taken control of Manchuria, renaming it Manchukuo. Kim said that he formed a small guerrilla group and began to engage in hit-and-run attacks against the Japanese. "I was so tense and excited that I could feel my heart beating," Kim recalled after one attack on a Japanese supply train.

During the struggle against the Japanese, four men called themselves Kim Il Sung. Among them was Kim Kwang-sŏ, who was educated by the Japanese but then tried to drive them out of Korea until his death in 1922. Kim Sŏng-ju also used the same name. He was educated in the Soviet Union, later became a member of the Chinese Communist army, and directed an attack against the Japanese in Korea in 1937. A third man who called himself Kim Il Sung might have

The father and predecessor of Kim Jong Il, Kim Il Sung was born a Korean patriot. Influenced by his parents and elders, Sung conducted passionate arguments against the Japanese occupation of Korea and soon became an ardent supporter of Communism. In the late 1920s, a 16-year-old Sung *(above)* even founded a Communist youth group.

directed a Communist assault on the Japanese in 1930. And the fourth person to use the name eventually became president of North Korea.

Kim's activities occurred in the rugged Antu area of Manchuria, in the same region as his family's home. While Kim was fighting the Japanese, his mother had become seriously ill. She died before he could return home from his campaigns.

During the early 1930s, the Communists were too weak to undermine Japan's occupation of Manchuria. Instead, Kim and his soldiers were forced to leave Antu and head to a new location along the mountainous border between Manchuria and the Soviet Union. Communist groups already operated in the area, but they were constantly being attacked by the Japanese.

Over the next few years, Kim led his men in raids against the Japanese. Along the way he earned a reputation as a hero of the resistance movement. Although some of the guerrillas were captured by the Japanese, Kim somehow escaped. Nevertheless, he was unable to drive back Japan's powerful armies, which controlled Manchukuo. By late 1940, Kim had left the area and moved to the safety of the Soviet Union. There he married another Korean, Kim Jong-suk. She was an attractive woman who had joined the guerrilla unit along with other women in the struggle against the Japanese. She sewed clothing and cooked for the guerrillas, while also serving as a member of the bodyguards who protected Kim. While living in the Soviet Union, the couple had two children—Kim Jong Il, known as Yura, who was born in 1942, and his younger brother, Shura.

KIM, KOREA, AND WORLD WAR II

While Kim had been living outside Korea, the Japanese had occupied the entire peninsula. New department stores had opened in Seoul and Pyongyang, but they were owned by Japanese merchants who controlled most of the business inside Korea. The Japanese opened new food processing plants, printing firms, chemical companies, and power plants. In the north, Japanese industrialists exploited large deposits of coal to run new factories and iron ore that was used to make steel. The

WHILE JAPAN'S RULERS INCREASED THE NUMBER OF SCHOOLS IN KOREA, THE BEST EDUCATION WAS RESERVED FOR THE JAPANESE STUDENTS.

increased production of steel was critical for Japan to build military weapons, such as tanks and planes, which could be used to extend its empire. Not only had the Japanese conquered Manchuria, they also controlled large areas of China.

Koreans were given jobs in the new Japanese enterprises but they were treated like second-class citizens. They were paid only half as much as the Japanese workers employed there. Meanwhile the Japanese increased taxes on Korean farmers and factory workers in order to bring more money into Japan's empire. While Japan's rulers increased the number of schools in Korea, the best education was reserved for the Japanese students. Korean students received an inferior education. Nevertheless, they were expected to swear their loyalty to the empire of Japan. Each elementary school student was required to recite a pledge to the Japanese emperor: "We are the subjects of the great empire of Japan. We shall serve the Emperor with united hearts. We shall endure hardships and train ourselves to become good and strong subjects."

Late in 1939, the Japanese government required Koreans to take another step in becoming subjects of the emperor. They were told to stop calling themselves by Korean names and adopt Japanese names. As a result, approximately 85 percent of the Korean population changed their names. As historian Andrew Nahm wrote, the Koreans "lost not only their national independence, but also their lands, their rights, and every aspect of their lives came under the control of Japanese rules and regulations."

On September 1, 1939, Nazi Germany invaded Poland, igniting World War II in Europe. Soon afterward, Japan entered into an alliance with Germany and began invading parts of

After escaping to the Soviet Union, Kim Il Sung married Kim Jong-suk, a woman dedicated to the guerilla movement to oust Japan from Korea. Known as the "Heroine of the Anti-Japanese Movement," she later gave birth to Kim Jong Il *(above, with his parents)* and his brother, Shura.

Southeast Asia. On December 7, 1941, Japanese planes struck the United States naval base at Pearl Harbor, Hawaii. This attack was followed by successful Japanese campaigns against the British colony of Singapore and American bases in the Philippine Islands.

While World War II raged across southern Asia, Kim Il Sung remained in the USSR, where he joined the Soviet army. He may even have been sent for special training to Moscow, where he rapidly proved to be an outstanding student. According to Yu Song-chul, who worked with Kim, he "was regarded as being exceptionally smart and possessive of leadership qualities. I believe this is why he was liked by the Soviets."

Although Japan and Germany had initially scored many victories, the tide of war gradually began to turn against them. By early 1945, both of these nations were near defeat at the hands of the United States and its allies—Great Britain, France, and the Soviet Union. In February, President Franklin Roosevelt met with Soviet dictator Joseph Stalin at Yalta inside the USSR. Roosevelt and Stalin agreed that Soviet forces should invade Manchuria, while the United States prepared for a final invasion of the Japanese islands.

In August, Soviet forces drove the Japanese out of Manchuria and marched south along the Korean Peninsula. In order to prevent the Soviets from occupying the entire peninsula, the United States convinced Stalin to agree to a division of the country along the 38th parallel that cut across the entire peninsula. This lies just north of Seoul and south of Pyongyang. Soviet forces occupied the northern part of Korea, while U.S. Army units took over the south. Meanwhile, the Japanese surrendered in August 1945, ending World War II.

NEW LEADER OF NORTH KOREA

The division of Korea created severe problems. Most of the coal used to power factories remained in the North, while the fertile rice-producing areas were located in the South. Most of the leading Korean politicians also lived around Seoul, which became the capital of South Korea. As the Soviets looked around for someone to lead the North, there seemed to be few choices among the Korean politicians. At first Soviet army commanders who led the invasion of Korea decided to support Cho Man-sik, a prominent Nationalist leader.

They also wanted Kim Il Sung—a loyal Communist—to have a leading role in Cho's new government. Kim and his family had returned to Korea with the Soviet armies. To strengthen his position inside North Korea, the Soviet commanders announced that General Kim Il Sung would deliver an important speech in Pyongyang. But the crowds who came to hear Kim were not impressed with him. Kim was only 33 and seemed too young to be a famous military leader, as the Soviets referred to him. As a result, the Soviets tried to build up Kim's reputation to make him more popular with the Korean people.

Meanwhile, a conflict had broken out between the Soviets and Cho Man-sik. Cho refused to run a government under the control of the USSR, demanding instead that Korea should be granted its independence. By early 1946, the Soviets had arrested Cho, and he was probably executed soon afterward. Meanwhile, Kim was prepared to work along with the Soviets and establish a Communist state in North Korea.

By late 1945, Kim had become head of the Communist Party in North Korea, with the support of the Soviet military authorities. He proved to be an effective leader whose personality attracted many followers, just as he had done during the war against the Japanese. From late 1945, when Kim took over control of the party, until August 1946, its membership grew from about 4,500 to 276,000. Anyone who did not agree with his leadership was rapidly removed by Kim. A year later, the membership had reached almost 700,000.

In February 1946, the Soviets selected Kim to become chairman of the Interim People's Committee—the new central government of North Korea. Under Kim's leadership, the government began to create a new army comprised mainly of people who had fought against the Japanese in China and Manchuria. Kim also began an extensive land reform program in North Korea. Land was taken from Korean aristocrats, Japanese landlords, and Buddhist temples and redistributed to peasant farmers. Each family received more than three acres for free from the new government. In addition, the Communist state took control of North Korea's industry. With financial aid from the USSR and the expertise of Soviet advisors, the economy began to grow, more people were employed in factories, and farms produced more crops.

북조선로동당중앙본부

Reluctant to trade Japanese soldiers for Soviet ones, Koreans at first did not accept Kim Il Sung as a potential leader of their nation. After the first USSR-chosen Korean leader demanded independence, he quickly disappeared and Kim rose to power. His portrait was soon carried through the streets of Pyongyang alongside the image of Stalin in a parade welcoming a U.S.-USSR commission.

By 1948, Kim established the Democratic People's Republic of Korea (DPRK). He appointed himself premier, the most powerful politician in the country. Kim was also head of the 800,000-member Korean Workers' Party (KWP)—the Communists. From its headquarters in Pyongyang, the party controlled every aspect of life in North Korea. Each town had its own small unit of Communists who reported directly to party headquarters on everything that happened in the community. Although Kim's parents attended a Protestant church, the new leader of North Korea had little interest in religion. Thousands of Christians who lived in North Korea fled to the South soon after Kim's takeover. Communists believed that Christianity had no role to play in a modern Socialist state.

In 1948, Kim established the Korean People's Army, a powerful fighting force that was supplied and trained by the Soviets. It included many Communist guerrillas who had fought alongside Kim in Manchuria as well as other veterans who had gained military experience in China. The army grew rapidly to a fighting force of 135,000 men supported by Soviet planes and tanks.

Kim Il Sung portrayed himself as the benevolent leader of North Korea—a father figure who was interested only in the welfare of his people. In this respect, Kim modeled himself after the Korean emperors of the past and the Japanese emperor who had ruled Korea for 35 years. Early in 1949, he began calling himself *suryong*, a term used by the Koguryŏ emperors that meant "great leader." In many ways, he was taking North Korea back to the future.

CHAPTER

4

The Korean War

KIM JONG IL GREW UP IN THE BUSTLING CITY OF PYONGYANG, WHERE HE had the good fortune of being the son of North Korea's most powerful leader. The younger Kim not only attended a fine elementary school where he had many playmates, he also had the companionship of his brother, Shura, and a younger sister. But Kim was a lonely child. In 1948, Shura drowned tragically in a pond near his family's home. A year later, Kim's mother was taken to the hospital, where she died shortly afterward.

In the meantime, Kim Il Sung was frequently away from home pursuing his dream of revitalizing North Korea and uniting it with the South. But to accomplish his goals he needed help from the Soviet Union. Kim Il Sung traveled to Moscow in early 1949, according to historian Allan Millett, where he "pressed his case with Soviet leader Joseph Stalin that the time had come for a conventional invasion of the South. Stalin refused, concerned about the relative unpreparedness of the North Korean armed forces and about possible U.S. involvement."

Kim Il Sung went back to Pyongyang, where he strengthened the Korean People's Army with the help of military aid from the Soviet Union. North Korean guerrillas were also operating south of the 38th parallel, hoping to undermine the government of South Korea. In Seoul, the capital of the Republic of Korea, South Korean leader Syngman Rhee had the same dream as Kim Il Sung—a unified Korea under a single government, but one led by Rhee. However, his army was much smaller than Kim's, and Rhee had to depend on American military forces to help him.

By 1949, American troops had withdrawn from South Korea, leaving its defenses much weaker. The following year, U.S. secretary of state Dean Acheson delivered a speech that defined America's "defense perimeter" in Asia to oppose the forces of Communism. Surprisingly, this perimeter did not include South Korea.

In March 1950, Kim Il Sung returned to Moscow, where he finally received Stalin's approval for an invasion of the South. However, the Soviet dictator told Kim that he had to have support from Mao Tse-tung, the leader of Communist China. When Mao agreed to back a North Korean invasion, Kim was ready to launch his troops into South Korea.

THE WAR OPENS

Early on June 25, 1950, more than 100,000 troops of the Korean People's Army crossed the 38th parallel and began their invasion. They rapidly overran the South Korean defenses and captured Seoul within three days. Although troops of the Republic of Korea tried to stop the North Koreans south of Seoul, they were heavily outnumbered and forced to retreat. Meanwhile, U.S. president Harry Truman realized that he had to move quickly before all of South Korea fell into the hands of the Communists. President Truman won the support of the United

During Kim Jong Il's early childhood, his father *(top row left)* often traveled to Russia and China in an attempt to gather military support for the reunification of Korea. Forces from the Korean People's Army in the North invaded the southern half of Korea in 1950 with the help of Stalin and Chinese Communist leader Mao Tse-tung.

Nations, which called on the North Koreans to stop their invasion. When Kim Il Sung refused, the UN agreed to assemble an international force, led by the Americans under the command of General Douglas MacArthur.

In the meantime, MacArthur sent a few troops from the American forces who were still occupying Japan after World War II. These troops, along with soldiers from the Republic of Korea, tried to hold back the invading North Koreans along the Kum River. But they were greatly outnumbered and driven back across the peninsula to a defense line north of the city of Pusan on the southern coast. In August, North Korean general

Kim Chaek led a bloody struggle aimed at finishing off the enemy. But by this time, American reinforcements had arrived and U.S. Air Force units had taken control of the air. As historian Michael Hickey wrote, "Throughout the war, air power was decisive. The North Korean air force was driven from the skies by US Air Force, Navy and Marines, using their superior equipment and training." Thousands of North Korean soldiers were killed or wounded, and their Soviet tanks were knocked out of action.

While the struggle was going on in the South, General MacArthur launched an amphibious invasion at Inchon, a port lying just west of Seoul. Led by the U.S. Marine 1st Division, American troops quickly overran North Korean defenders at Inchon and headed inland, entering Seoul on September 25. After fierce house-to-house fighting against troops of the Korean People's Army, the Marines finally took control of the city. Caught between American forces in Seoul and Pusan, the North Koreans rapidly retreated. But along the way, the Korean People's Army was almost destroyed.

"As the communists headed north," according to Millett, "they took thousands of South Koreans with them as hostages and slave laborers, and left additional thousands executed in their wake." Approximately 5,000 South Koreans were executed at Taejon. Meanwhile, U.S. airplanes bombed the retreating North Korean forces, killing many innocent civilians along the way.

THE WAR ENTERS A NEW PHASE

As North Korean troops fled northward across the 38th parallel, General MacArthur demanded that Kim Il Sung surrender. Instead, Kim ordered his soldiers to "fight to the end." Meanwhile, MacArthur and President Truman agreed that U.S. forces should cross into North Korea and try to unify the peninsula under the control of President Rhee. In early

October, MacArthur led his troops across the 38th parallel toward Pyongyang.

As these forces approached the capital city, Kim Jong Il and his sister became part of the retreating line of Koreans heading northward. According to author Choe In Su, the car in which they were riding traveled along a road that was "packed with people streaming northward. . . . The going was possible only at night, otherwise in the daytime enemy planes would raid." Their first stop was a mountainous area near the Yalu River. But as the American invasion continued, Kim and his sister were taken across the border into China. Here he attended school, possibly near Jilin, where his father had lived many years earlier.

As the retreat was under way, Kim Il Sung had already sent an urgent request to the Chinese to assist the North Koreans. Two of his associates journeyed to Beijing, where they met with Mao Tse-tung and other Chinese leaders in October 1950. They were informed that the Chinese had decided to enter the war and drive back the American armies. Mao feared that a unified Korea under President Rhee with the support of U.S. troops would be a threat to the Communist government in China. Mao also had the backing of Stalin, who promised to provide Soviet planes to drive the U.S. air forces out of the skies.

On October 25, 1950, South Korean forces fighting along-side the Americans encountered Chinese troops that had crossed the Yalu River. The Koreans were defeated by the Chinese, who then launched an attack against U.S. troops in the area, driving them southward. Many of the attacks came at night, when the Chinese could operate under the cover of dark-ness, ambushing American soldiers and destroying their sup-plies. But after a brief campaign, the attacks suddenly stopped. MacArthur believed that the Chinese drive had ended, and he ordered his troops to continue northward.

By this time, the harsh Korean winter had already started, and U.S. supply lines were stretched almost to the breaking

Although U.S. soldiers were able to drive Kim Il Sung's forces out of Seoul and southern Korea, they were unprepared for the Chinese forces they faced in the Battle of Chosin Reservoir. An estimated 25,000 American troops faced a full-out attack of more than 125,000 Chinese soldiers in ice-cold conditions *(above)* and managed to stop the enemy surge.

point. Late in November, the Chinese struck again in over-whelming numbers, pushing U.S. forces southward toward Pyongyang. Fortunately, American planes still controlled the air, and their F-86 Sabre jets proved to be too much for the Soviet-made MiGs. The American air force "turned its fury on all standing structures that might shield the Chinese from the cold; cities and towns all over North Korea went up in flames," according to Allan Millett.

WHILE THE WAR ACCOMPLISHED VERY LITTLE, AN ESTIMATED 3.5 MILLION KOREANS HAD LOST THEIR LIVES.

Nevertheless, the Chinese army of more than 400,000 troops succeeded in driving the combined South Korean and U.S. forces out of North Korea and even succeeded in recapturing Seoul by early January 1951. As the war continued during the rest of the year, MacArthur's forces gradually pushed the Chinese out of Seoul and back to a position just north of the 38th parallel. By this time, the conflict had reached a stalemate, with more than one million soldiers in the combined Chinese-North Korean forces facing almost 800,000 on the other side. Secret talks between the United States and the Soviet Union finally led to the beginning of peace negotiations in July 1951. Meanwhile, U.S. airplanes carried out extensive bombing raids over North Korea, as battles were fought between American forces and the Chinese armies.

Fighting continued into 1953, as negotiators talked at P'anmunjom, a North Korean village. Both sides accepted a line near the 38th parallel as the border between North and South Korea. An agreement was finally signed on July 27, 1953, by the United Nations and North Korea. It included a three-mile-wide (4.8 kilometers) demilitarized zone around P'anmunjom. This area was patrolled by a force of neutral United Nations soldiers and North Korean soldiers.

IMPACT OF THE WAR

Although the Korean War had finally ended, it did not turn out the way that Kim Il Sung had planned. Instead of unifying Korea under his control, he remained the leader of only North Korea, which was located within approximately the same borders as before the war. While the war accomplished very little, an estimated 3.5 million Koreans had lost their lives. Among these were about 129,000 South Koreans who had been massacred by the Korean People's Army. Thousands more had been kidnapped by the North Korean soldiers, separated from their families, and forced to travel north to serve the army.

The Korean People's Army itself had suffered over 500,000 casualties while fighting the war. Meanwhile, an estimated 2 million North Koreans—almost one-quarter of the population—had lost their lives during the warfare on the ground and the terrible bombing raids. Another one million North Koreans had decided to leave the North and live in South Korea. Pyongyang and many other towns had been burned to the ground, farms and factories had been destroyed, and the entire economy lay in ruins.

While Kim Il Sung had completely miscalculated the launching of the invasion of South Korea, he refused to take responsibility for the disaster. Instead he tried to blame his subordinates, who, he claimed, had not done their job properly. To prevent any members of the Communist Party from mounting a challenge to his leadership, he began to remove anyone who opposed him or his conduct of the war. Some members were driven out of North Korea, while others were executed.

Meanwhile, Kim Il Sung claimed that he had successfully driven back an invasion of North Korea, saving his country from the South Koreans and the United States. On July 28, 1953, the People's Assembly of North Korea declared that Kim was a hero of the Democratic People's Republic of Korea. Kim was given a special medal because he had "organized and led the Korean people and the People's Army to a shining victory in the Fatherland Liberation War, with his outstanding strategy and tactics."

5
The Development of North Korea

WHEN KIM JONG IL RETURNED TO PYONGYANG AFTER THE KOREAN WAR, HE found his father's capital devastated by bombing raids that had changed the entire city. Changes had also occurred in the boy's family. Kim Il Sung had decided to marry again—this time to an attractive secretary named Kim Song-ae who worked in one of the government offices. In 1953, she gave birth to a son named Kim Pyong-il. Kim Jong Il was convinced that his father and new mother did not love him as much as his stepbrother. Kim did not like his stepmother, and conflicts developed between them that continued for many years.

In the meantime, Kim Il Sung had very little time to spend with his family because he had taken on the enormous task of revitalizing North Korea after the war. One of Kim Il Sung's main concerns was the education of the Korean people. Before the Communists came to power, most Koreans were unable to read or write, and only a relatively small number of children attended elementary school. Kim Il Sung had begun building new schools before the war, and this effort continued during the 1950s. North Korean children were offered a free education by the government, and most of them began attending school.

The curriculum in the public schools included the Korean language, mathematics, art, and music. But children also spent part of their time learning about the "Great Kim Il Sung, Communist values, and Communist Party Policy," according to author Donald Seekins. Although schools were open to everyone, the best instruction was reserved for the children of Communist leaders. A similar policy had existed during the years of Japanese occupation when government officials who ruled the country sent their children to the best schools in Korea. Kim Jong Il attended Pyongyang Primary School No. 4 and Nasman Senior Middle School.

One of the policies that children learned about was called *chuch'e*. This was a North Korean brand of Socialism developed by Kim Il Sung. According to historian Bruce Cummings, "*chuch'e*, which means placing all foreigners at arm's length," appealed strongly to "Korea's Hermit Kingdom past. *Chuch'e* doctrine stresses self-reliance and independence [and] after Kim took power, virtually all North Koreans were required to participate in study groups and re-education meetings, where regime ideology was inculcated."

The concept of chuch'e is also based on the historical traditions of Confucianism. It emphasizes a hierarchical form of society, with the Great Leader—Kim Il Sung—at the top. He was the benevolent father, the ideal leader, described by Confucius. According to author Don Oberdorfer, "the Great Leader is the brain that makes decisions and commands action, the Workers Party is the nerve system" that carries these decisions to all North Koreans, "and the people are the bone and muscle that implement the decisions and channel feedback to the leader."

STATUES OF KIM WERE ERECTED IN NORTH KOREAN COMMUNITIES, AND BY THE 1960S, EVERY NORTH KOREAN WORE A PIN WITH A PICTURE OF THE NATION'S LEADER.

Kim Il Sung was at the nation's center, and the people worshipped him. His picture was on a wall in every home, and it appeared in schoolrooms across the nation. Statues of Kim were erected in North Korean communities, and by the 1960s, every North Korean wore a pin with a picture of the nation's leader.

While North Koreans admired their Great Leader, they also feared him. Kim Il Sung established a large force of secret police agents who examined mail at the post office and did not hesitate to wiretap anyone suspected of not supporting the government. These agents relied on a large number of paid informants who reported any person who might seem the least bit suspicious. Any North Korean who did not support Kim's policies would be forced out of the country, executed, or imprisoned. Perhaps as many as 150,000 people were held in one of North Korea's prison camps. As Professor Dae-Sook Suh wrote, Kim was "a ruler who wields more power than the notorious monarchs of the old Korean kingdom."

THE RECONSTRUCTION EFFORT

As soon as Kim Il Sung returned to Pyongyang, he began an effort to rebuild his war-torn nation. Huge construction projects that employed large numbers of North Koreans were undertaken in cities like Pyongyang. Dams that were destroyed by bombing raids during the war had to be rebuilt. These dams not only provided a steady stream of water for irrigation projects that were needed for North Korean farms, but also served as a source of hydroelectric power. Water turned enormous turbines that in turn created electricity to light cities and run factories. The rebuilding projects employed large numbers of North Koreans, giving them a steady income after the end of the Korean War.

Although Kim Il Sung believed in self-sufficiency and going it alone, he was not opposed to receiving foreign aid. Most of it came from his Communist allies, the Soviet Union and China. They helped finance the reconstruction projects and the industrialization that began to occur across North Korea. While most people had worked in agriculture before the war, gradually a larger and larger number of North Koreans began to be employed in industry.

At first, the focus was on so-called heavy industry. Factories manufactured tractors for use on farms and chemical fertilizers designed to improve crop yields, as well as cement and turbines for hydroelectric power plants. In addition, the government tried to increase the amount of coal dug from the mines in mountainous regions of the country. Coal was used to power electric plants that lit homes and ran factories. Kim Il Sung also emphasized the importance of mining iron, which was turned into steel to build machines for North Korean factories.

Control of the economy was centered in the State Planning Committee. Staffed by loyal members of the Communist Party, these experts determined how much each industry should produce. The State Planning Committee set targets in five-year and seven-year plans. They also decided on the supply of raw materials and financial resources that should be given to each factory. But problems began to occur because the State Planning Committee made mistakes in determining the amount of resources needed by each factory. As a result, factories sometimes failed to meet their targets. Kim Il Sung tried to deal with these problems by giving bonuses to factory workers, including free vacations and special medals if they met their goals.

Kim Il Sung was a tireless administrator who toured the country, visiting factories and power plants to find out how successfully they were operating. He realized that problems were arising and decided to change the system of industrialization. He began the Tae-an work system, a team approach to manufacturing. One team included the factory manager and a group of engineers. They supervised the day-to-day operation of a factory. Another team, headed by a committee of the Communist Party, located in each facility, made sure that the factory met its production goals. Unfortunately, this created too much bureaucracy in each manufacturing plant and failed to improve efficiency.

REFORMS IN AGRICULTURE

Kim Il Sung not only emphasized industrialization but improvements in North Korean agriculture. He hoped to make his nation self-sufficient in food. This was a difficult task because North Korea contains relatively few areas with a climate for growing wheat, corn, and rice. These are located along the coast and in the regions around Pyongyang. In the past, the North had depended on the South for supplies of rice because South Korea contains a much larger area suitable for agriculture.

After coming to power, Kim Il Sung had redistributed land and given farms to the North Korean peasants. But after the Korean War, he began to follow a Soviet model of agriculture. This meant eliminating private property and combining the individual farms into large cooperatives. These were created around villages in the countryside. Peasant families living on the cooperatives worked together, buying animals and farm implements, planting crops, and harvesting them. Irrigation projects, fertilizers, and better seeds were provided by the government to increase crop production.

While there was adequate food in the countryside, the cooperatives did not meet the targets set by Communist planners for the entire country. Especially in the cities, food had to be rationed. Consequently, there was insufficient rice and grain to satisfy the needs of many North Koreans. However, the Communist elite, like Kim Il Sung and his family,

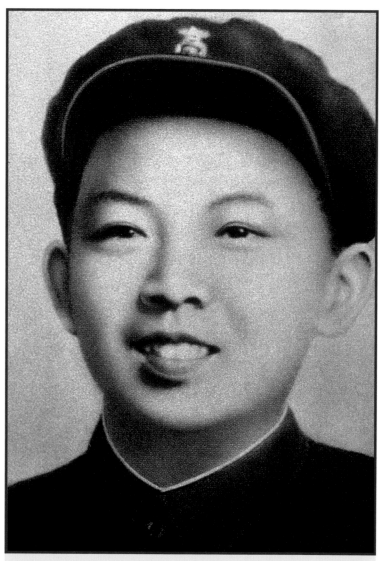

As the son of Korea's most powerful man, Kim Jong Il *(above)* received the best education available to him. While not much is known about his formative years, it has become common knowledge that his younger brother drowned in an accident, his mother passed away in childbirth, and his father was usually working abroad in Russia. Kim Jong Il experienced upheaval during the Korean War, when he was relocated to safer areas of Manchuria.

received as much food as they wanted. While many North Koreans ate no meat, it was readily available to the families of the Communist leaders. They also lived in the best houses. Peasants and workers had small, two-room homes and apartments with tile roofs. The Communist elite had spacious one- and two-story houses.

INCREASING THE NORTH KOREAN MILITARY

During the 1960s, Kim Il Sung began to spend more and more money building up the North Korean army. By the early 1970s, the army had grown to more than 400,000 troops according to author Don Oberdorfer. About 15–20 percent of the economy was devoted to the military. Indeed, it was described as "perhaps the most highly militarized society in the world." Experts disagree on Kim Il Sung's reasons for this decision. Some believe that he had decided to make another attempt at invading South Korea and uniting the two nations under his control. Others suggest that Kim feared that South Korea, with the backing of the United States, might decide to invade the North. By this time, South Korea had been taken over by a military government, headed by Park Chung Hee. The United States had also become more heavily involved in a conflict between Communist North Vietnam and the government of South Vietnam.

Whatever the reason for Kim Il Sung's decision to expand the military, it had a huge impact on the economy. Consumer goods had never been widely available in North Korea because the government was focused on heavy industry. Indeed, all the stores were operated by the Communist government. These included some department stores, vegetable and meat markets, and some shops in towns and villages. Factories also ran outlets where North Koreans could buy items such as clothing. Nevertheless, the selection of consumer goods was limited.

During the 1960s, the quantity of consumer goods declined even further. Meanwhile, North Korean factories focused more of their efforts on producing military weapons. More and more male workers were serving in the armed forces, reducing workers who were available to be employed in factories and agricultural cooperatives.

This was one of the reasons why Kim Il Sung urged women to leave home and enter the workforce. They were necessary to replace men who had gone into the military. The government also promoted the development of state-run nurseries, called *t'agasos*. There were approximately 8,000 of them by the late 1960s. Parents could place their children in the t'agasos each day when they were only a few months old. The nurseries continued to take these children until they had reached age four. Then they went to kindergarten and later elementary school. After-school programs were also provided by the government. Children could enroll in the Pioneer Corps and the Socialist Working Youth League. The league ran large halls with libraries, museums, gymnasiums, and theaters. These not only offered lectures and poetry readings; children were also taught the principles of Communism and chuch'e.

THE RISE OF KIM JONG IL

Those students who graduated from high school and performed well on admission exams attended Kim Il Sung University, which was started in 1946. This was the only college that provided a full range of undergraduate and graduate programs. Kim Jong Il and many of his friends attended this university after they left secondary school. Kim Jong Il's friends described him as a young man who was accustomed to being considered better than his classmates because he was the son of the North Korean leader. "He was a perpetual showoff," one of them said. "He was self-centered and his behavior was impolite. He used to boast of his high-quality watch to other classmates. Frequently he had fun driving a car or motorbike at a fast speed in the streets of Pyongyang."

Kim Jong Il majored in political economy. But he often let other students know that he thought that he was smarter than his professors. Instead of studying, however, Kim spent much of his time in college enjoying parties and romantic relationships with women on the campus. Nevertheless, he also gained a reputation as someone who would take time off from enjoying himself to help fellow students, especially if they were sick.

During his adolescence and college years, the five-foot, two-inch Kim sometimes accompanied his father on political tours. In 1959, he went to Moscow with Kim Il Sung. Kim Jong Il also took trips to towns across North Korea to visit the sites of his father's battles against the Japanese in the years before taking power. And in 1963, he traveled with his father to a military camp near the Demilitarized Zone (DMZ).

After his graduation from college, Kim Jong Il went to work in the Central Committee of the Korean Workers' Party. His responsibility was to help supervise the propaganda created by the party to glorify Kim Il Sung. After a short time in this position, Kim Jong Il was assigned to the military unit in charge of guarding his father. This enabled him to accompany Kim Il Sung on more inspection tours to steel mills and other factories.

After serving in the bodyguard, Kim Jong Il was reassigned to the Central Committee of the KWP. As part of the effort to turn his father into a godlike ruler, Kim Jong Il had small sculptures of Kim Il Sung mass-produced and distributed to study halls in schools across North Korea. He supervised a new collection of his father's writings about chuch'e, and arranged tours so that North Koreans could visit the locations of Kim Il Sung's victories over the Japanese.

Promoted to director of propaganda in the Central Committee, Kim Jong Il devoted much of his time to North Korean filmmaking. He insisted that all films should reflect the writings of his father, and art and literature should embody the values of chuch'e. Kim Jong Il directed filmmakers to concentrate on movies that portrayed his father's guerrilla campaigns against the Japanese during the 1930s. In the late 1960s, he worked closely with writers to develop a script for one of these films, called *Sea of Blood*. It was directed by Kim Jong Il and released in 1969. Kim was also involved in the production and editing of other films in the 1970s, including *The Fate of a Self-defense Corps Man, The Flourishing Village,* and *The Worker's Family.*

In 1972, Kim Jong Il was placed in charge of the celebrations for his father's sixtieth birthday. As part of the events, he supervised the writing of a special song that paid tribute to Kim Il Sung titled "Long Life and Good Health to the Leader." He also supervised the development of new acts performed by the Pyongyang Circus for his father's birthday gala.

Two years later, Kim Jong Il was already being considered by the Central Committee as Kim Il Sung's successor. One of his jobs was to lead teams of young Communist Party members, known as Three Revolution Teams, into factories and onto collective farms. There they were expected to raise the level of enthusiasm among the workers and increase production. They were also ordered to root out any officials who did not enthusiastically support the ideals of the Communist revolution in North Korea. Many young college graduates wanted to join the teams and work directly for Kim Jong Il because they realized that it would help their own careers.

Members of the Communist Party also showed their support for Kim Jong Il by giving him expensive gifts. And Kim enjoyed purchasing pricey gifts for them in return. This was part of his luxurious lifestyle, one that was only available to a tiny number of people. Kim reportedly enjoyed heavy drinking parties with other elite members of the party as well as the company of attractive women. His first marriage to Hong Il-chon, the daughter of a Communist Party member, had ended in divorce. In 1973, he married Kim Yong-suk, a typist who worked for the government. She was selected for him by his father, Kim Il Sung.

But Kim Jong Il also enjoyed relationships with other women, including the beautiful actress Sung Hae-rim. In 1971, Sung and Kim had a son, named Kim Jong-nam. Sung and her son lived in one of the magnificent mansions that Kim maintained for himself in North Korea. At age 10, Kim Jong-nam was sent to Geneva, Switzerland, where he attended an exclusive school. Along with him went his cousin, Li Nam-ok, who had lived with Kim and his mother. As a member of the Kim family, Kim Jong-nam had to be well educated because he was recognized as a possible leader of North Korea, following his father and grandfather.

KIM JONG IL'S RESPONSIBILITIES GROW

Meanwhile, Kim Jong Il was dealing with problems within the Communist Party. Because of his quick rise to the top as the son of the North Korean leader, Kim had earned the envy of other members of the KWP. Some of them felt that he was unqualified for a leadership role. Senior officials who had served with his father in the guerrilla wars against the Japanese felt that Kim Jong Il was far too young for a leadership position. But those who were openly critical of him were quickly arrested and thrown into prison.

Others resented his style of management. While Kim Il Sung was warm and outgoing, his son did much of his work in secret. He was far more critical than his father of the efforts by Communist officials to carry out the economic and social programs of the government. Hwang Jang Yop, a top official who left North Korea in the late 1990s, said that "Kim Jong Il is by nature a person who does not like living in harmony with others. He makes people fight against each other and depend only on him." During the meetings where managers were encouraged to criticize each other "even the smallest defect [in carrying out a program] is blown out of proportions into a serious incident." Hwang added that Kim is very secretive, "and has cruelly killed countless people. His worst

As he grew into adulthood and began to work with government officials, Kim Jong Il's *(center)* leadership abilities were doubted and feared. The skeptics, however, remained quiet because they did not want to be thrown into prison for being disloyal.

fear is having these crimes exposed," which accounts for much of his secretiveness.

During the 1970s, Kim Jong Il became head of internal security for North Korea. In this position, he increased the number of people imprisoned by the regime and built more prison camps. As author Jasper Becker wrote, "The political prisoner camps became so large that Kim Jong Il turned them into a vital pillar of the planned economy, an army of slaves who produced nearly all the food and goods consumed by the Party's elite. Yodok, the name of the No. 15 [camp] . . . holds about 50,000 prisoners who work at a gypsum quarry, a gold mine, a textile factory, a corn distillery, and a coppersmith workshop. The inmates also raise rabbits whose fur is used to line soldiers' winter coats . . . Camp No. 25 builds refrigerators and . . . bicycles with which the regime rewards its most loyal followers, and Camps Nos. 14 and 22 supply Pyongyang's elite and its hotels with 100,000 tons of meat a year."

Ahn Myong-chol, a former prison guard in North Korea, recalled that, at one of the prison camps, the inmates were "walking skeletons of skin and bone. Their faces were covered by cuts and scars where they had been struck. Most had no ears; they had been torn off in beatings." If one person seemed disloyal to the government, his entire family would be imprisoned in the same camp. Nevertheless, the disloyal member was separated from the rest of his family and not allowed to communicate with them.

FOREIGN AFFAIRS

During the 1960s, incidents along the DMZ were becoming more common. From 1967 through 1969, 38 American soldiers patrolling the DMZ were killed by North Korean guerrillas and many more were wounded. Some South Korean troops also lost their lives. In 1968, Kim Il Sung sent a group of commandos into South Korea, where their mission was the murder of President Park. But word of the mission reached the police in Seoul, who intercepted the commandos before they could reach the president's home, killing most of them.

During the same year, North Korean ships intercepted the American reconnaissance ship *Pueblo*. The *Pueblo* had been sent to observe North Korean coastal defenses and to intercept military communications. North Korean ships fired on the *Pueblo*, wounding Commander Lloyd Bucher and three of his sailors. Bucher and the rest of the ship's crew were captured by the North Koreans, charged with spying by government authorities, and imprisoned. North Koreans tortured Bucher until he finally signed a confession admitting that he and his crew had come to spy on the Communist regime. Eventually, after almost a year in prison, the crew was released.

In 1976, a group of 15 men, including Americans and South Koreans, were working in the DMZ. Directed to prune a tall poplar tree, they had just begun when a unit of the KPA appeared, consisting of several officers and enlisted men. The commander of the unit ordered the Americans and South Koreans to stop their work, warning that "if you cut more branches, there will be a big problem." When his warning was ignored, the North Korean commander called for reinforcements. Then he made an even harsher statement: "The branches that are cut will be of no use, just as you will be after you die." When the Americans continued working, the KPA soldiers attacked. The American in charge of the unit, Captain Arthur Bonifas, was "beaten to death by five or six North Koreans wielding clubs," according to Don Oberdorfer. His second-in-command, Lieutenant Mark Barrett, was also killed. Soon American reinforcements arrived, and the North Koreans retreated. U.S. president Gerald Ford considered a military strike against North Korea in response to the deaths of the American soldiers, but he decided not to act, fearing that it might lead to another war on the Korean Peninsula.

Meanwhile, U.S. involvement in Vietnam had come to an end with the withdrawal of all American troops. By this time, most Americans had grown tired of their country's involvement in foreign wars. In 1976, they elected Democrat Jimmy Carter as president. Carter favored a withdrawal of U.S. troops from the Korean Peninsula. He believed that there was general military equality between North Korea and South Korea, so the Seoul government had nothing to fear from Pyongyang. But American intelligence reports during the Carter administration indicated that the size of North Korea's army had greatly increased. Indeed, these reports suggested that Kim Il Sung had expanded his army from almost 500,000 troops to almost 700,000. This made it much stronger than the South Korean forces.

As a result, American plans to leave South Korea were abandoned, and U.S. troops remained on the Korean Peninsula. In 1979, President Park Chung Hee was assassinated. Following the assassination, and the instability of the South Korean government, the Carter administration feared that Kim Il Sung might decide the time had come to launch another invasion of the South. But nothing happened. Nevertheless, tensions would continue to grow during the 1980s.

CHAPTER

6

The Struggles of the Kim Il Sung Regime

IN 1980, KIM IL SUNG MADE AN OFFICIAL ANNOUNCEMENT THAT HIS SON, Kim Jong Il, would be his successor as head of the North Korean government. Meanwhile, the younger Kim had also become a secretary—that is, a leader—of the Communist Workers' Party. He was known as the Dear Leader to distinguish him from his father, the Great Leader. Portraits of the Dear Leader and the Great Leader appeared side by side inside government buildings in Pyongyang and throughout the rest of North Korea. The North Korean people also displayed pictures of both leaders in their homes.

Although Kim Jong Il had achieved enormous power in North Korea, he continued to work behind the scenes and did not show himself in public very much. He rarely met with foreign heads of state who came to North Korea, and he rarely traveled abroad. Kim Il Sung still served as the public leader of North Korea, but during much of the 1980s, his son was actually running the government. To prepare North Koreans for the day that Kim Jong Il would take over from his father, Communist officials began to build up the younger Kim's public image. A museum portraying his accomplishments had already been built in Pyongyang, but new elements of his life suddenly began to appear.

Although Kim Jong Il had been born in the USSR, his official birthplace was changed to a location in North Korea that seemed more appropriate for a Korean leader. The site selected was a former guerrilla camp operated by his father near Mount Paektu, the highest peak in North Korea. Kim was also praised for his work with the Three Revolution Teams and his efforts to transform the North Korean economy.

Meanwhile, Kim Jong Il was also trying to distinguish himself as a movie producer. Kim is a devoted movie fan, with thousands of films reportedly stored in his library. He was eager to increase North Korea's prestige by producing award-winning films. To help him accomplish this goal, Kim decided to bring a famous South Korean director, Shin Sang-ok, to the North. Kim's agents first kidnapped Shin's former wife, the highly successful actress Choi Eun-hi when she was visiting Hong Kong in 1978. After she arrived in Pyongyang, Kim gave her a beautiful home and an expensive car. Although Choi did not know why she had been kidnapped, it eventually became apparent to her. Shin, who had continued to be fond of his wife after their divorce, tried to find Choi after her disappearance. This led him to Hong Kong, where he was grabbed by North Korean agents. When he refused to remain in North Korea and tried to escape, Shin was jailed. Finally, he agreed to write a letter to Kim Jong Il apologizing for his conduct. Eventually, Shin was released, and in 1983, he was reunited with his former wife. Shin then went to work directing films in North Korea in a multimillion-dollar studio built by Kim. Shin and Choi were permitted to travel abroad to publicize the films. At first, they were heavily guarded, but when they convinced Kim of their loyalty, he removed the guards. In 1986, they escaped and never returned to North Korea.

THE LAGGING ECONOMY

While Kim spent millions on film production, the North Korean economy continued to lag during the 1980s. Instead of improving industrial production, a large amount of money was spent on building up the military. In addition, the North Korean government had focused much of its remaining resources on huge projects that failed. Among these was an expensive dam, called the West Sea Barrage, started in 1981 and finished five years later. The main purpose of the dam was to irrigate several hundred thousand acres of saltwater tidelands along the coast that were to be transformed into productive farms. This supported the government's chuch'e program leading to self-sufficiency in food production. But after the barrage was completed, the government never followed through on the plan to expand the nation's farmland, and very little tideland actually became productive farms.

Another plan called for the development of a new vinalon plant. Vinalon was a chemical fiber used to make clothing and shoes. Instead of cotton, which was difficult to grow in North Korea, the chuch'e program of self-sufficiency substituted vinalon. In the 1950s, this was produced from coal and limestone, both easily available in North Korea. The new plant called for even greater production. As by-products, the plant was also designed to produce large quantities of fertilizer and food for farm animals. But after the plant was begun at huge cost, it was never completed. A third very expensive project was a fertilizer complex, designed to increase crop production. But this complex also failed to be completed.

Meanwhile, food shortages in the North continued to grow during the 1980s. By this time, Kim Jong Il was directly in charge of the government, so he was blamed for the problem. Not only was grain and rice being rationed for Korean civilians, soldiers in the armed forces were also short of food. According to Lee Min-bok, a food expert who escaped from North Korea, the rationing grew much worse by the mid-1980s. People were supposed to receive food every two weeks at large distribution centers, but the rations frequently failed to arrive on time.

In an interview with author Jasper Becker, Lee explained that North Korea "ran short of a million tons of food each year, enough to feed around three million people. The leadership never grasped the extent of the unfolding disaster because no one dared tell Kim Il Sung the truth. 'Everyone knew how to please the Great Leader—all you had to do was lie. So what people did was to cheat by making false reports. Say a party official had to meet a target of 100 tons of grain, and the real harvest was 70 tons, he would report that he had met the quota.'" The regime had tried to increase food production by resorting to terrace farming. Plots were laid out on the many hillsides in North Korea. But each year when the heavy rains came, the soil and the crops were washed away.

In 1984, severe floods occurred in South Korea, destroying a large part of the food crops. To score a propaganda victory and to show the world the success of its own farm program, the North Korean government offered to send rice to the South. But this decision only increased the hardships for the North Korean people, who were already desperately short of rice for their own families.

In one area, however, Kim Jong Il had managed to achieve some economic success. On August 3, 1984, a fair featuring North Korean consumer goods was held in Pyongyang. Displayed at the fair were products such as furniture, stationery, and athletic equipment manufactured by local factories from scrap material left over from their manufacturing operations. Some of the products were also produced by teams of

After the fall of the USSR and its allies in Eastern Europe, North Korea experienced shortages in energy, food, and general goods. Because gas is limited, the streets throughout the country are often empty. However, traffic directors are still required to fulfill their duties to support a façade of prosperity *(above)*.

people working from their homes. Kim praised the items that he saw at the fair and encouraged an expansion of the August Third program, as it was called.

The idea began to spread across North Korea. Stores started opening in many towns and counties, where local officials could set prices. In the past, according to author

Hy-Sang Lee, the central government had established the same price for the same product throughout North Korea. "Under this seemingly fair but unnatural policy of ignoring transportation and storage costs," prices were the same in Pyongyang where a product was manufactured and in a county hundreds of miles away. As a result, there was very little incentive to open local stores because no profit could be made. "Now with the new authority to sell August Third goods in direct sales stores under the control of the county, local officials had more discretion in setting prices . . . bringing prices better in line with costs."

Nevertheless, the North Korean economy continued to struggle. In 1986, author Jasper Becker visited Pyongyang. As his car headed toward the capital, he noticed that the highway was almost empty of cars. There was too little gasoline to run them. The subway stations inside the city were bright and clean, but hardly ever used. "The inhabitants' chief role," he wrote, "is to take part in mass demonstrations of support, and they are constantly in training to perform at some military parade, celebration, or demonstration. . . . You find the same familiar sights as in any big city—department stores, grocery shops, smart hotels, bars, restaurants, and hospitals—but nothing as mundane as shopping or eating goes on in them. From the outside a grocery store looks normal. The windows and glass counters are clean and hygienic, the vegetables are in the baskets, the tins of meat on wooden shelves, and the condiment [spice] bottles are laid neatly in rows. Yet there is nobody there. No one is shopping, and no one ever will. Nothing is actually for sale because when you look closely the vegetables are all made of plastic. . . . On a tour of the maternity hospital, it is the same. The rooms, full of new, modern medical equipment, are for show too. Not even the plastic wrapping on the electrical plug for the . . . heart monitor has been removed."

To show off the power of North Korea, Kim sent his agents to kidnap citizens of Japan and South Korea.

NORTH KOREA AND THE WORLD

While he was dealing with the problems of North Korea's economy, Kim Jong Il was also running North Korea's foreign affairs. To show off the power of North Korea, Kim sent his agents to kidnap citizens of Japan and South Korea. These people were taken to prison camps in North Korea, where they disappeared. As a way of boosting its lagging economy, North Korea had also become a major supplier of arms to other nations, especially in the Middle East. These weapons included tanks, short-range missiles, and missile launchers to countries such as Iraq, Libya, and Syria.

In 1982, Kim had launched an assassination plot aimed at South Korea's president, Chun Doo Hwan. The following year, Chun and senior members of his government were visiting Rangoon, the capital of Burma (now called Myanmar). Some of them had already arrived for an official ceremony at the capital, but Chun was running behind schedule. As the South Korean officials prepared for Chun's arrival, a bomb suddenly exploded, killing four of them. The bomb had been planted by a North Korean army officer, Zin Mo, and several other agents. They were later caught and confessed that the bombing had been planned by the North Korean government.

President Chun and his U.S. allies feared that the assassinations might be followed by North Korean military action along the Demilitarized Zone. Indeed, some members of the president's cabinet wanted to bomb North Korea. But Chun refused to allow any attack. Indeed, in 1984, secret talks had begun between North Korea and South Korea aimed at improving relations between the two countries. They were conducted by Park Chul Un, a South Korean diplomat and an expert in foreign affairs, and Han Se Hae, a leading North Korean diplomat.

The two men hoped to lay the foundation for a summit meeting between Kim Il Sung and Chun Doo Hwan. But there were too many disagreements between the two sides, and the secret talks finally ended. The North Korean government was especially upset by a military training exercise, called Team Spirit, that was scheduled for 1985. Kim Jong Il believed that this exercise, which involved thousands of U.S. and South Korean troops, posed a threat to his father's regime.

To deal with any threats that might arise from the South, Kim Il Sung visited Moscow in 1984, where he persuaded Soviet leaders to send additional fighter planes to North Korea. As in the past, the Soviets wanted to maintain a close relationship with Korea, which they considered an important ally in the Far East. In 1986, Kim Il Sung returned to the Soviet Union, where he received additional fighter planes.

That same year, the Great Leader, according to historian Alexandre Y. Mansourov, experienced a major heart attack and fell into a coma. North Korean doctors were unable to revive him. Therefore, his son, Kim Jong Il, approached the Soviet ambassador and explained that "the Great Leader was passing away from us." He added that "we badly need urgent medical assistance from the Soviet cardiologists [heart doctors]." The ambassador sent an urgent telegram to the Soviet leader, Mikhail Gorbachev, and less than a day later, 15 Soviet cardiologists landed in Pyongyang. In two days of medical treatments the doctors successfully revived Kim Il Sung and he returned to his duties as the Great Leader of North Korea.

Although the Soviets had saved the life of Kim Il Sung, this did not stop them from changing their policy toward North Korea. As the economy in the North grew weaker, the South Korean economy was becoming one of the most successful in

Asia. Meanwhile Soviet leader Mikhail Gorbachev had begun a policy of opening up the USSR to new trade relationships with capitalist economies, including South Korea. However, Kim Il Sung was opposed to any Soviet plans to open trade talks with South Korea, fearing that these might undermine Gorbachev's support for the North Korean government.

North Korea's leaders were also concerned about the impact of the 1988 Olympics that began in Seoul on September 17. Athletic teams from around the world, including many from Communist countries, gathered for the event, which was telecast to an enormous global audience. The huge expense of building the facilities for the Olympics showcased South Korea's economic success for the entire world. During 1986, North Korea had approached the South Korean government about sharing the Olympics. Kim Il Sung wanted half the events in North Korea, but the South Koreans agreed to let the North host only the table tennis and fencing contests. When North Korea refused this compromise, the talks between the two countries ended.

Meanwhile, Kim Jong Il had developed a plan aimed at frightening athletes so they would not fly to the games in Seoul. In November 1987, two North Korean agents were sent to Baghdad, Iraq, where they boarded South Korean Air Flight 858. After placing a bomb on the plane, they left the flight in Abu Dhabi. After the flight took off, the bomb exploded, killing all the passengers.

One of the agents, Kim Hyon Hui, was eventually caught by police and flown to Seoul. Under intense questioning, she finally admitted to participating in the plot. She later told author Don Oberdorfer that she had been told that the bombing "was for unification of the country." But gradually, Kim realized that "I had just committed the crime of killing compatriots. . . . Finally, I decided I had to tell the truth." Following eight days of denying any involvement in the bombing, she said: "Forgive me. I am sorry. I will tell you everything." Shortly

Kim Hyon Hui *(right)*, a North Korean agent who planted a bomb on a South Korean airliner, confessed her crimes in Seoul, saying her orders came directly from Kim Jong II. In her confession, Kim told authorities a kidnapped Japanese citizen held in North Korea instructed her on Japanese mannerisms to offset suspicion.

afterward, the United States announced that it had decided to treat North Korea as a terrorist state.

HARDSHIPS INCREASE IN NORTH KOREA

Shortly after the end of the Seoul Olympics, the Soviet Union, led by Gorbachev, decided to strengthen its relations with South

Korea. The driving force behind this decision was money. Trade relationships with South Korea could improve the Soviet economy. South Korean business leaders had also shown an interest in investing money in new projects located in Siberia and other parts of the Soviet Union.

Kim Jong Il opposed Gorbachev's decision, but he had little to offer the Soviets. Since the Soviet economy was weak, Gorbachev needed to make every effort to strengthen it. This eventually led him to embrace the policy of perestroika, opening up the economy to limited amounts of capitalism. Gorbachev's trade relationships with South Korea were part of his effort to revitalize the Soviet Union economically. As Gorbachev himself put it, "We will firmly proceed on the way to . . . establishing relations with South Korea. We are now taking this necessary decision."

On January 1, 1991, Gorbachev established full diplomatic relations with South Korea. Up until this time, the USSR had recognized only North Korea as the legitimate government of the Korean Peninsula. Gorbachev's decision, combined with weakening economic conditions in the Soviet Union, changed the situation in North Korea. In the past, the Soviets had provided crucial oil supplies to North Korea as well as weapons and industrial machinery. These had been sold at specially reduced prices, and the Soviets had even allowed Kim not to pay for much of what he had received.

Suddenly, this special relationship had changed. Oil supplies to North Korea were reduced by 75 percent. Since part of the oil was used in chemical fertilizer, farm production was affected. Gasoline supplies were also reduced for tanks and airplanes. Kim Jong Il turned to China, which had also supplied North Korea with oil. But the Chinese refused to supply oil at the low prices offered in the past by the Soviets. When Don Oberdorfer visited North Korea in 1991, he noticed "deserted roadways and idle construction projects" around Pyongyang.

There was no gasoline to run automobiles or heavy construction equipment.

In 1992, the Chinese also decided to establish diplomatic relations with South Korea. This decision, along with the changing policies in the Soviet Union, left Kim Jong Il and his father feeling more and more isolated in North Korea. As a result, they turned to a new strategy—one designed to get the attention of their former Communist allies as well as the rest of the world.

THE NUCLEAR OPTION

During the mid-1980s, North Korea had begun receiving nuclear reactors from the Soviet Union. These were designed to enable the development of nuclear power for generating electricity. At the same time, Moscow required Kim Il Sung to join the Nuclear Non-Proliferation Treaty. Begun in 1968, it committed the nations that signed the treaty to stop the spread of nuclear weapons. But while Pyongyang agreed to the terms of the treaty, it was secretly developing a nuclear weapons program. U.S. surveillance satellites had photographed the buildings involved in the program at Yongbyon, north of Pyongyang, as early as 1982. The nuclear facilities included a reactor, and a few years later, a partly completed reprocessing plant. This might have given the North Koreans the capability of separating plutonium from nuclear fuel and building an atomic bomb.

The nuclear weapons program was directed by Dr. Lee Sung Ki, a close friend of the Great Leader. Kim Il Sung and his son believed that as their economy declined a nuclear bomb might force the major world powers to pay attention to North Korea. This would put the Communist regime on an equal footing with the United States, China, and the USSR, each of which had nuclear capability. In addition, it would give North Korea the power to control events on the Korean Peninsula.

DEALING WITH NORTH KOREA

In 1988, Republican George H.W. Bush was elected president of the United States. Bush believed that the North Korean nuclear weapons program posed a threat to world peace. He also realized that the United States had to work together with the other major powers to force North Korea to dismantle its nuclear facilities. Nevertheless, Kim Jong Il and his father refused to permit inspectors from the International Atomic Energy Agency (IAEA) to enter North Korea and inspect the facilities at Yongbyon. The United States had nuclear missiles below the DMZ to defend South Korea, and Kim Il Sung refused to dismantle his nuclear operations until these were also removed.

To reduce tensions on the Korean Peninsula, Bush decided to remove the nuclear missiles. Soon afterward, meetings began to be held between diplomats from North Korea and South Korea in Pyongyang. The North Korean leaders had been under intense pressure from China and Russia to begin talking to the South Koreans. Meanwhile South Korean president Roh Tae Woo seemed eager for a summit meeting with Kim Il Sung where the two men could resolve their differences. In 1991, both sides issued a joint declaration agreeing to recognize each other's governments. They also declared their intention to replace the armistice that had ended the Korean War with a genuine peace agreement and not to use force against the other. At the end of the year, both nations also agreed not to "test, manufacture, produce, receive, possess, store, deploy or use nuclear weapons," and to permit inspections.

In 1992, the IAEA sent inspectors into North Korea to examine the facilities at Yongbyon. Although the North Koreans stated that they had only been separating plutonium in 1990, the inspections indicated that North Korea was lying to the inspectors. Additional work had probably been going on to develop a nuclear weapon. A new crisis developed that seemed to undermine the earlier agreement. Meanwhile, South Korea

Despite signing a treaty promising not to create nuclear weapons, surveillance information soon revealed that Kim Jong Il had disregarded the agreement. Satellite photos of Yongbyon, North Korea (above), clearly show an area in development for nuclear facilities, ones that one day may provide materials for nuclear weapons.

announced that it planned to resume the Team Spirit exercises, which had been stopped to promote peace. This decision angered Kim Jong Il and his father. In 1993, the South Koreans became upset when they uncovered a Communist spy ring, probably directed by Kim Jong Il.

Tensions increased even more when satellite photos confirmed that the North Koreans had a much larger nuclear weapons facility than they had admitted. But Kim Jong Il and his father were unwilling to admit that this facility existed. This would have meant losing what the Koreans called *ch'emyon*, or respect, in the eyes of the world. "For us, saving face is as important as life itself," one North Korean official explained. In the meantime, Kim Jong Il, who had been named commander in chief of the North Korean armed forces in 1991, put them on a war alert. North Korea also withdrew from the Nuclear Non-Proliferation Treaty.

While war seemed a real possibility, secret talks were under way between representatives of the United States and North Korea. Many of these conversations took place in an out-of-the-way coffee shop in New York City—a location where the press would be unlikely to see anything and write about it. Eventually, the North Koreans permitted the IAEA inspectors to return, but they were not allowed to examine all the nuclear facilities. As Don Oberdorfer put it, "If it was established that Pyongyang had not diverted nuclear fuel [secretly] to manufacture plutonium in the past, its nuclear threat would diminish and with it the country's bargaining power; but if the [inspections] established that Pyongyang had lied and produced more plutonium than it had admitted, it would lose face."

While the crisis continued, U.S. president Bill Clinton, who had taken office in 1993, ordered additional missiles to South Korea. In response, Kim Jong Il directed his military leaders to ready missiles to defend Pyongyang. In 1994, Clinton sent additional troops to South Korea and planned to hold the Team Spirit exercises. But, as the conflict grew worse, the Clinton administration received a message from former president Jimmy Carter that he was planning to visit Kim Il Sung in Pyongyang. Carter's mission was to try to conclude a peace agreement. While serving as president in 1978, Carter had negotiated a peace treaty between Israel and Egypt, two countries that had been at war for decades. After leaving the White House in 1981, the former president had set up the Carter

Center, an organization dedicated to finding peaceful solutions to international conflicts.

As Carter traveled to North Korea, Kim Il Sung and his son were under intense pressure from China to come to an agreement and avoid war. After arriving in Pyongyang in mid-June, Carter was warmly greeted by Kim Il Sung. The presence of an American leader of Carter's stature for the first time in Pyongyang convinced Kim Il Sung that North Korea was receiving the recognition that he wanted.

After some hard bargaining with President Carter, Kim Il Sung agreed to halt the nuclear weapons program and to permit IAEA inspections. In addition, Kim had decided to hold a summit meeting with the South Korean president. But on July 7, 1994, before the summit could begin, Kim Il Sung was on one of his inspection tours. The tour apparently exhausted him, and the Great Leader suffered a heart attack, dying early the next morning.

Kim Jong Il had suddenly become the new leader of North Korea.

7

In the Shadow
of His Father

"THE GREAT HEART STOPPED BEATING," WAS THE MESSAGE BROADCAST over Radio Pyongyang—the government-controlled station— on July 8, 1994. North Koreans were stunned by the news. For many of them, Kim Il Sung was the only leader they had ever known. On a hill, overlooking the center of Pyongyang, the Great Leader had built an enormous statue of himself. Here, thousands of people who had heard the news gathered tearfully to recall the man who had guided their country for 50 years.

Shortly after Kim Il Sung's death, the Communist Party held a magnificent funeral for the Great Leader in Pyongyang. While the elite members of the party praised his accomplishments, the Dear Leader, Kim Jong Il, said nothing at the ceremony. He stayed in the background, much the same role he had played during his father's rule.

Yet, for at least 15 years, Kim Jong Il had governed North Korea jointly with his illustrious father. While the Great

Leader was the public face of the country, the Dear Leader focused on the details of running the day-to-day operations of the government. He often worked far into the night, preparing comprehensive reports for his father on the state of the military and the condition of the North Korean economy. But it is not clear whether he included all the information that reflected the real state of affairs. While the economy declined, Kim Il Sung seemed to know very little about how poorly fed many North Koreans really were because of his economic policies.

In the years leading up to his father's death, Kim Jong Il had moved many of his relatives, friends, and associates into positions of power. His sister, Kim Kyong Hui, was a high-level industrial manager while her husband, Chang Song Taek, was one of the Dear Leader's closest advisors. The husbands of his stepsisters—the daughters of the Great Leader's second wife— also held high government and military positions.

A NUCLEAR DEAL

Although his father had died, Kim Jong Il continued negotiations with the United States over the North Korean nuclear facilities. At Geneva, Switzerland, U.S. negotiators pressed for inspections of the operations at Yongbyon. But Kang Sok Ju, leader of the North Korean negotiating team, continued to refuse. Nevertheless, both sides wanted to make a deal. The United States wanted to reduce the nuclear threat from North Korea, and Kim Jong Il needed nuclear reactors to produce electric power. Finally, U.S. negotiators, led by Robert Gallucci, forged an agreement with the North Koreans. Known as the Agreed Framework, it called for inspections to be delayed until the nuclear reactors were delivered—probably five years away. The United States agreed to deliver fuel oil to North Korea each year until the reactors began operation and to "provide formal assurances against the threat or use of nuclear weapons against North Korea."

When Kim Il Sung died suddenly in 1994, thousands of North Koreans attended a massive funeral ceremony in Pyongyang *(above)*. The years of isolation and propaganda in North Korea contributed to the myth of the man people came to know as the "Great Leader."

The North Koreans were pleased with the deal, but the South Koreans were critical of it. They realized that by negotiating face-to-face with North Korea, the United States had given recognition to the Communist regime. Indeed, the Agreed Framework called for the United States and North Korea "to open diplomatic liaison offices in each other's capitals as initial steps toward eventual full normalization of relations." The United States had also convinced South Korea to provide nuclear reactors to the North. But the Clinton administration and the Japanese agreed to pay for them.

Shortly after negotiations between North Korea and the United States were concluded, a crisis occurred along the Demilitarized Zone. A U.S. helicopter with two army officers

on board mistakenly flew a few miles into North Korean terri-
tory. The helicopter was shot down by DPRK planes, and one
of the officers, Chief Warrant Officer David Hileman, died in
the crash. However, the other officer, Chief Warrant Officer
Bobby Hall, was captured by the North Koreans. Negotiations
led to the release of Hileman's body, but the North Korean
government refused to free Hall. Kim Jong Il called on the
United States to continue negotiations. Kim was hoping that
he could get a U.S. commitment that would lead to a formal
peace treaty and diplomatic recognition. But U.S. negotiators
refused to agree to anything except "sincere regret" for the
"legally unjustified intrusion into DPRK air space." North
Korean negotiators took this statement to Kim Jong Il, who
eventually "approved" it. He overruled his military leaders,
who were more concerned about a violation of North Korean
air space than they were about maintaining improved relations with the United States after the Agreed Framework.
When one of the American negotiators, Thomas Hubbard,
received word of Kim's decision, he recalled, "I became convinced that there was a supreme being there, and that probably it is Kim Jong Il."

ECONOMIC DISASTER

While Kim was consolidating his power, North Korea was
struck by one of the greatest natural disasters in the history of
the Communist regime. On June 26, 1995, heavy rains struck
the country, with as much as 18 inches (45.72 centimeters)
falling in one day. The rains caused tremendous flooding that
washed away homes and destroyed large areas of croplands.
"Rain was three to five times the normal level," according to
historian Bruce Cummings. "By the time the storms stopped
in mid-August, the North Korean government said that some
5.4 million people had been displaced . . . 1.9 million tons of
grain lost, with the total cost of the flood damage pegged at
$15 billion."

Kim Jong Il was forced to make a desperate appeal to the United Nations for aid. The UN agreed to provide assistance but only if its workers were permitted to enter North Korea and supervise the distribution of the aid. While Kim did not want Western observers traveling across his country, he had to agree. A UN official reported that he saw "people scavenging in the fields looking for roots and wild plants to prepare soup for their families. People were anxious, restless. They are not getting enough to eat."

But the UN also reported that the agricultural program in North Korea had been encountering problems even before the floods struck. The collective farms established by Kim Il Sung had been producing far too little food to feed the North Korean people adequately.

In addition to aid from the UN, North Korea received assistance from the United States and other nations. Stewart Greenleaf and Robert Egan were two of the people who went to North Korea, bringing food and other supplies. "We carried humanitarian aid with us on the plane, and had some of it shipped—baby food, medicines, vitamins," Greenleaf said. He recalled visiting a hospital where a surgery procedure was under way. "The patient was awake and he had his coat on, because it was so cold." Heating fuel and electricity were scarce. "I was traveling on a train," Egan said, "and it would stop often because it ran out of electricity, and so I'd get out and look at the different villages, which were very remote and impoverished." He added: "I noticed in every cornfield . . . a raised stand, with a guard." Egan asked someone about them and was told that they were "protecting the corn from people coming out in the middle of the night and stealing it."

In the North, food rations had been severely reduced to only 1,000 calories a day, about one-half the minimum requirements set by the United Nations. Somehow, most people managed to survive, but they soon were forced to deal with a new crisis.

Natural disasters such as intense flooding and severe drought in the 1990s hindered North Korea's food production, plunging the country into a state of starvation. During this famine, more than one million people died from starvation, and many children, such as the nursery school students *above*, were left permanently stunted by the lack of food. The situation has not improved; a 2008 report by the World Food Program and the United Nations declared that 40 percent of North Korea's young children were chronically malnourished.

In 1996, heavy rains again struck North Korea, and these were followed by a severe drought in 1997. More than one million people may have perished from starvation—about 5 percent of the North Korean population of 20 million. Kim's government continued to ask the United Nations for food supplies. The United States also offered to provide some assistance, but U.S. political leaders were not willing to do too much to help what they considered to be a brutal regime. When Kim said that he would accept the aid only if it were tied to peace talks and recognition from the United States, the United States refused. Kim was forced to back down and take food supplies any way he could get them.

Not only was food in short supply for North Korean civilians, it was also in short supply among the soldiers in the North Korean army. According to author Jasper Becker, "Kim Jong Il sent soldiers directly to the farms at harvest time to forcibly grab the harvest. Consequently, by the autumn of 1997, rural households were down to just 220 pounds of grain per person, not enough to last the whole year." Becker added that the people did everything possible to deal with the situation. Grain was hidden from the government and sold illegally on the black market. In the cities, people began planting small gardens in their yards and raising rabbits for food. "Officials told people to collect roots, bark, seaweed, husks, and cobs to make noodles or 'cakes,' food with no caloric [nutritional] value." The people "often died when their [stomachs and intestines] failed to process the dense matter."

Some families tried to leave their villages and escape across the border into China. Many of these refugees were rounded up by the North Korean police and put into camps where they received very little food. Those few who crossed the border soon discovered that the Chinese did not want refugees inside their country. They were arrested by police and returned to North Korea.

Some of these refugees reported that political conditions inside North Korea had become unstable. In 1995, a plot by some members of the army had been discovered and stopped. The plotters planned to take over the port of Chongjin, then attack Pyongyang and overthrow Kim Jong Il and his government. That same year, North Koreans tore up pictures of Kim and his father that were hanging at the Nakwon machinery plant in the city of Sinuiju.

KIM DID NOT COMMAND
THE SAME LOYALTY AND RESPECT
GIVEN TO HIS FATHER.

Although Kim Jong Il was protected by a large bodyguard, refugees said that he had been the target of an assassination attempt in 1998. Kim did not command the same loyalty and respect given to his father.

In February 1997, for example, Hwang Jang Yop, a close advisor to Kim Il Sung and Kim Jong Il, defected to South Korea. The 74-year-old Hwang had helped develop the chuch'e philosophy, which lay at the foundation of the North Korean economy. He had also served in the Supreme People's Assembly and as a secretary of the Workers' Party. Hwang regularly traveled to Beijing, the capital of China, on economic missions. While visiting there, he had begun making contacts with South Koreans during 1996. Reportedly Hwang was concerned that under Kim Jong Il the DPRK military was becoming far too powerful. He feared that a war might break out on the Korean Peninsula. Hwang said that Kim Jong Il "worshipped Germany's [Adolf] Hitler [leader of the Nazi Party] from an early date and wanted to become such a dictator as Hitler. . . . He considers the party and military as his own and does not care about the national economy." While Hwang continued to support the North Korean regime outwardly, he secretly began planning his escape. Visiting Japan early in 1997, he delivered several speeches about chuch'e and the North Korean leadership. From Japan, Hwang flew to Beijing, where he supposedly planned to go on a shopping trip. But on February 12, he entered the South Korean embassy and asked for protection. Eventually the South Koreans flew him to Seoul. The defection of such a high-level Communist leader was very embarrassing to Kim Jong Il's government. As Hwang said in a written statement, "At a time when workers and farmers are starving, how could we consider people sane who loudly say they have built an ideal society for them?"

As the economic situation worsened, Kim looked for scapegoats to blame. In 1998, the government executed the agriculture minister, So Kwan-hi, and others who were held responsible for the food shortages. A year later, Kim's son, Kim Jong-nam, led a military force looking for people who were smuggling goods across the Chinese border in exchange for food. Some of them were rounded up and publicly shot to send a message to any other North Koreans who might try the same thing. But the smuggling continued as people openly defied the government. Unless Kim could find a solution to the nation's economic problems, his grip on power might gradually weaken.

8

Kim Jong Il and the World Stage

IN JUNE 2000, KIM JONG IL MET WITH THE PRESIDENT OF SOUTH KOREA, Kim Dae Jung, in Pyongyang. This was the first summit meeting between the leaders of North Korea and South Korea since the peninsula was divided. The meeting was part of Kim Dae Jung's Sunshine Policy. This was designed to "actively push reconciliation and cooperation between South and North," as Kim explained it. During the early years of his leadership, Kim Jong Il had continued to work behind the scenes, never speaking or appearing in public. The summit marked the first time that he had publicly entered the international arena. According to author Hy-Sang Lee, Kim was "gracious" and "courteous" to his guest, Kim Dae Jung.

As a result of the summit, the two leaders issued a joint declaration calling for a settlement of "Korea's reunification at the earliest possible date based on the three principles—independence, peaceful unification and great national unity . . .

[in] a federal state of the nation." The summit was part of an effort by South Korea to provide additional economic aid to the North as a way of improving relations. Whether Kim Jong Il ever meant to carry through on a peaceful confederation or closer ties with the South is doubtful, according to author Gordon Chang. At the same time, North Korea was continuing to supply missiles to other nations. Kim Jong Il was also secretly developing his own nuclear weapons.

In part, this may have been a response to worsening relations with the United States. Since the Agreed Framework had been signed, little had happened. The delivery of the nuclear power plants was behind schedule. The oil supplies that the United States was supposed to send to North Korea were also late. Finally, the Agreed Framework had called for "improved relations" with the United States. But there had been no improvement. As Deputy Assistant Secretary of State Charles Kartman put it, "There are reasons why the North Koreans might think we weren't totally sincere."

Kim Jong Il had tried to force the United States to pay attention to him by offering to stop producing ballistic missiles if the Clinton administration carried out the Agreed Framework. When this did not work, Kim had tested a long-range ballistic missile over the Sea of Japan in 1998. Finally, after the summit with South Korea, there was an effort by the Clinton administration to restart talks with Kim Jong Il's government. In October 2000, Vice Marshal Jo Myong Rok, a top North Korean leader, met with American diplomats in Washington. They agreed that "neither government would have hostile intent toward the other." This was followed by a trip to Pyongyang by Secretary of State Madeleine Albright. She met with Kim Jong Il, who said he would consider putting an end to the manufacture and export of all missiles. Kim hoped that President Clinton would come to North Korea to follow up on the meeting and sign an agreement. When this did not occur, Kim made no effort to stop missile production.

In a historic meeting, South Korean president Kim Dae Jung *(left)* and Kim Jong Il met for the first time ever to discuss attempts to reconcile the two Koreas. This summit was the first political and international appearance of Kim Jong Il since he took charge of North Korea after his father's death.

NORTH KOREA AND THE BUSH ADMINISTRATION

In 2000, Republican George W. Bush was elected president of the United States. After coming to office, the Bush administration reviewed the past American relationship with North Korea. As a result of this review, the administration said it was ready to continue talks with North Korea but only after Kim

KIM BELIEVED THAT HIS MISSILES AND HIS NUCLEAR CAPABILITY GAVE HIM IMPORTANT BARGAINING CHIPS IN HIS DEALINGS WITH THE UNITED STATES.

Jong Il stopped all missile production. President Bush did not mention the nuclear reactors that had never been delivered to North Korea. He insisted that IAEA inspectors should immediately be permitted to inspect North Korea's nuclear facilities. Bush feared that nuclear weapons in the hands of Kim Jong Il were a grave threat not only to the Korean Peninsula but to the safety of the world. The Bush administration also feared that the DPRK might not stop at producing short-range missiles, like the ones that were being sold to nations in the Middle East. Instead, Kim Jong Il's regime might be developing long-range ballistic missiles that could potentially strike the U.S. mainland.

North Korea immediately refused President Bush's terms. Kim believed that his missiles and his nuclear capability gave him important bargaining chips in his dealings with the United States. Without these chips, Kim feared that U.S. hostility toward North Korea, reaching back to the Korean War, might eventually lead to another conflict and the overthrow of his regime.

RELATIONS WITH OTHER NATIONS

Although talks with the United States had stalled, North Korea was pursuing relationships with other nations. New economic agreements were signed with South Korea. The amount of trade between the two nations had risen from $425 million in 2000 to $642 million by 2002. Since the summit meeting in 2000, a series of reunions had also occurred between Korean families separated after the peninsula was divided into two countries. Approximately 8,000 Koreans had been permitted to reunite for short meetings with family members.

In 2002, there were talks in Pyongyang between Kim Jong Il and Japanese prime minister Junichiro Koizumi. Prime Minister Koizumi wanted to establish diplomatic relations with North Korea. Koizumi was also willing to provide reparations—as much as $10 billion to North Korea for the damage inflicted on the country by the Japanese during World War II. In return, Kim admitted that North Korean agents had kidnapped Japanese citizens in the 1970s and 1980s. He also agreed to return the kidnap victims who were still alive. But the Japanese people were outraged that their leader should give reparations to a government that had admitted kidnapping Japanese citizens. As a result, Koizumi ended his diplomatic negotiations with Kim as well as his offer of $10 billion.

AXIS OF EVIL

Meanwhile, relations with the United States had declined even further. On September 11, 2001, agents of the international terrorist organization known as al Qaeda hijacked several American planes. These struck the World Trade Center in New York and the Pentagon in Washington, D.C., killing thousands of people. In retaliation, the Bush administration declared a "War on Terror" aimed at striking international terrorist organizations wherever they were operating. In January 2002, President Bush delivered his "axis of evil" speech, mentioned in chapter one, naming North Korea, Iran, and Iraq as three governments that were hostile to the United States. The president also announced a new U.S. policy of starting a preventive war against any nation that might possess weapons of mass destruction. This policy was designed to destroy those weapons before they could be used against the United States or the rest of the world.

Throughout 2002, the Bush administration focused most of its attention on Iraq. But the efforts of Prime Minister Koizumi of Japan to begin talks with North Korea eventually led to discussions by the United States and North Korea in October 2002. These were tough talks, and Assistant Secretary of State James Kelly accused North Korea of continuing a secret nuclear arms program. According to author Leon V. Sigal, the "next day North Korean negotiator Kang Sok Ju acknowledged its existence. That was at once a threat to develop nuclear arms and an offer to stop. Kelly made it clear Washington did not want further talks: the North had to stop, or else."

Sigal added, "North Korea had resumed production of plutonium by refueling and restarting its reactor at Yongbyon, which had been frozen under the 1994 Agreed Framework. The reactor can generate a bomb's worth of plutonium in a year. Allowing at least another six months to reprocess and weaponize the plutonium, it could have a nuclear device in a year and a half, another device a year or so later, or five to six in six years."

Kim Jong Il may have hoped that by admitting the existence of his nuclear operations he could persuade the Bush administration to provide economic aid to North Korea, just as President Clinton had done under the Agreed Framework. When the Bush administration refused to deal with North Korea, Kim stubbornly refused to back down. Meanwhile, in early 2003, the United States and its allies launched a war against Iraq. This war sent a signal to North Korea that it could be next.

"In its official reaction to the start of the Iraq war, North Korea noted that the United States had first demanded that Iraq submit to inspections, and it did," Sigal wrote. "The United States then demanded that Iraq disarm, and it began to. The United States then attacked it anyway." A North Korean Foreign Ministry official added, "This suggests that even the signing of a non-aggression treaty with the U.S. would not help avert war. Only military deterrent force, supported by ultra-modern weapons, can avert war and protect the security of the nation. This is the lesson drawn from the Iraqi war."

ECONOMIC REFORMS IN NORTH KOREA

By using nuclear weapons as a bargaining chip, Kim Jong Il hoped to get a peace treaty with the United States that included financial aid for his country. North Korea had just begun a series of economic reforms as a result of the problems encountered during the 1990s. In part, the reforms also occurred because of pressure from China, North Korea's ally. The Chinese had already reduced control of the economy by the government and encouraged free enterprise, which led to an enormous economic boom. In 2002, Kim began to move his economy in the same direction.

Among the earliest changes, the government no longer controlled the price of rice, an important food in the North Korean diet. As a result, the price of rice increased by 550 times. The rising price encouraged farmers to plant more rice and harvest larger crops. Meanwhile, the farmers were permitted to open more markets where they could sell the produce that was grown on their private farm plots. As prices increased, the government also boosted wages by 60 times the current levels.

Unfortunately, the rise in wages and prices produced enormous inflation across North Korea. Although people had far more money, it was worth far less. Poor North Koreans with little money suffered in the new economy. At the same time, the government stopped handing out rations of food, which hurt the poor even more severely.

But some North Koreans benefited from the new economy. Farmers with crops to sell could make a larger income than they had previously enjoyed. In addition, the government encouraged the establishment of small businesses in towns and cities across the country. Some of these businesses were run by women. As the state-run factories had run short of fuel and electricity during the 1980s and 1990s, many workers had been laid off. As Gordon Chang wrote, "In many households women became the sole source of sustenance. . . .

JANUARY 13, 2003

www.time.com AOL Keyword: TIME

TIME

THE BIGGER THREAT?

KIM JONG IL

NORTH KOREA'S dictator is a nuclear menace.
Why he may be more dangerous than Saddam

$3.95US

This 2003 *Time* magazine cover surrounds an image of Kim Jong Il with nuclear warheads as the headline ominously warns of potential trouble. By using his nuclear capabilities as leverage, Kim has managed to eke out aid deals with Western nations. He walks a dangerous line with these tactics, as any military conflict would threaten food production and the North Korean economy.

Today, many of these homegrown . . . businesses are flourishing." A small middle class began to develop in North Korea. Some people, according to Chang, became successful enough to afford expensive automobiles and designer clothing with fancy labels.

Among the most successful North Koreans were high-ranking members of the military. The armed forces developed "powerful trading companies," according to Bruce Cummings. "These firms handle commercial exports of the North's abundant minerals (gold . . . coal)." In addition, the companies may also be involved in an illegal drug trade in opium.

At the same time, manufacturing firms from South Korea began to develop plants in the North. At Kaesong, located just across the border from Seoul, the Hyundai group was developing a new economic zone where firms from South Korea would do business in the North. These economic programs were so new that it was impossible to measure their success during the first decade of the twenty-first century. Nevertheless, the growth of the North Korean economy will be critical to Kim Jong Il's long-term success as the ruler of his country.

Kim's success will also depend on his relations with the major world powers, including China, Russia, and the United States. Continued military buildup and nuclear confrontations, like the one that occurred in 2006–2007 will only continue to undermine the economic growth of North Korea. Nevertheless, Kim feels that his country is threatened, especially by the United States. This fear is based on North Korea's long history, which has included invasions by China, Russia, and Japan, as well as the United States. A willingness by North Korea to disarm its nuclear arsenal as well as desire by the United States to improve its relations with the regime of Kim Jong Il may be the only solution that can begin to bring a lasting peace.

CHRONOLOGY

12th century B.C.	Pyongyang becomes capital of Choson kingdom.
108 B.C.	China invades Korea and establishes colonies.
4th century A.D.	Kingdom of Koguryŏ arises.
7th century	Shilla becomes main kingdom in Korea.
10th century	Koryŏ becomes dominant kingdom in Korea.
13th century	Mongols conquer Korea.
1392	Yi dynasty begins and rules Korea until 1907.
1871	U.S. troops invade Korea.
1875	Japanese troops invade Korea.
1880s	Japan and China vie for control of Korea.
1893	Peasant revolt breaks out in Korea.
1894	Sino-Japanese War begins; Japan takes control of Korea.
1904	Russo-Japanese War begins over control of Korea.
1907	Japan annexes Korea.
1912	Kim Il Sung is born.
1914–1918	World War I rages across Europe.
1919	Kim Il Sung and his parents move to Manchuria.
Late 1920s	Kim Il Sung organizes resistance groups against Japanese.
1930	Kim Il Sung is arrested in Manchuria.
1931	Kim Il Sung joins Chinese Communist Party; fights Japanese.

1939–1945	World War II occurs.
1940	Kim Il Sung moves to Soviet Union.
1942	Kim Jong Il is born.
1945	Korean Peninsula is split between North Korea and South Korea; Kim Il Sung becomes head of Communist Party in North Korea.
1948	Kim Il Sung establishes Democratic People's Republic of Korea.
1950	North Korea invades South Korea to begin Korean War.
1953	Korean War ends.
1960s	Kim Jong Il attends Kim Il Sung University.
1968	*Pueblo* incident occurs.
1973	Kim Jong Il marries Kim Yong-suk.
1976	Incident occurs along Demilitarized Zone.
1980	Kim Jong Il is named successor to Kim Il Sung.
1983	North Korean agents try to assassinate South Korean president.
1987	North Korean agents bomb Korean Air Flight 858.
1988	Seoul Olympics occur in South Korea.
1991	USSR establishes diplomatic relations with South Korea. Kim Jong Il becomes commander in chief of North Korean army.
1992	China establishes diplomatic relations with South Korea.
1994	Kim Il Sung dies; Kim Jong Il becomes leader of North Korea.

1996–1997	Floods and drought strike North Korea.
1998	North Korea tests long-range missile over Sea of Japan.
2000	Summit meeting between leaders of North Korea and South Korea.
2002	President George W. Bush delivers "axis of evil" speech. North Korea begins economic reforms.
2006	North Korea detonates nuclear explosion.
2007	North Korea agrees to shut down nuclear facilities; Summit meeting between leaders of North Korea and South Korea.

BIBLIOGRAPHY

Becker, Jasper. *Rogue Regime: Kim Jong Il and the Looming Threat of North Korea.* New York: Oxford University Press, 2005.

Chang, Gordon. *Nuclear Showdown: North Korea Takes on the World.* New York: Random House, 2006.

Cummings, Bruce. *North Korea, Another Country.* New York: The New Press, 2004.

Koh, Byung Chul, ed. *North Korea and the World.* Seoul, South Korea: Kyungnam University Press, 2004.

Martin, Bradley. *Under the Loving Care of the Fatherly Leader: North Korea and the Kim Dynasty.* New York: St. Martin's Press, 2004.

Savada, Andrea, ed. *North Korea: A Country Study.* Washington, DC: Library of Congress, 1994.

FURTHER READING

"America's Wars: The Major Events of the Korean War."
History Central.com. Available online:
http://www.historycentral.com/korea/index.html.

Behnke, Alison. *North Korea in Pictures.* Minneapolis, MN:
Lerner Publications, 2005.

Haberle, Susan. *North Korea: A Question and Answer Book.*
Mankato, MN: Capstone Press, 2005.

Hickey, Michael. "The Korean War: An Overview." BBC
History. Available online: http://www.bbc.co.uk/history/
worldwars/coldwar/korea_hickey_print.html.

"Kim Il Sung." Encyclopedia Britannica. Available online:
http://www.britannica.com/eb/article-9115499/Kim-Il-Sung.

Kummer, Patricia. *Korea.* Danbury, CT: Children's Press, 2004.

WEB SITES

BBC, "The Korean War: An Overview"

http://www.bbc.co.uk/history/worldwars/coldwar/korea_hickey_print.html

Federation of American Scientists, "Plutonium Production"

http://www.fas.org/nuke/intro/nuke/plutonium.htm

HistoryCentral. com, "America's Wars,"

http://www.historycentral.com/korea/cn_message.html

PHOTO CREDITS

INDEX

ABOUT THE AUTHORS

RICHARD WORTH is the author of more than 50 books, including the Chelsea House titles *Independence for Latino America, Dalai Lama, Dolores Huerta*, and *Gangs and Crime*, which was selected to the New York Public Library's Books for the Teen Age list in 2003.

ARTHUR SCHLESINGER, JR. is remembered as the leading American historian of our time. He won the Pulitzer Prize for his books *The Age of Jackson* (1945) and *A Thousand Days* (1965), which also won the National Book Award. Schlesinger was the Albert Schweitzer Professor of the Humanities at the City University of New York and was involved in several other Chelsea House projects, including the series *Revolutionary War Leaders, Colonial Leaders*, and *Your Government*.

9/06

mL